In 1992, Michoel Levy left his career as a barrister to find where life would take him. It took him across Europe, seeking out and reviving the ancient arts of the travelling storyteller. For five years, he lived on the road, telling his stories on bridges, in parks and in town squares. Now, he spends his time with his family, studying the Babylonian Talmud and, of course, telling stories.

The cover drawing is by Darren Baker, who was the official portrait artist of Her Majesty The Queen in 2011, the official artist to the 2012 Olympic games, and whose works grace the collections of 10 Downing Street, The House of Lords, St James's Palace and the Bahrain Royal household.

Michoel Levy

THUNDER ROSE

AUSTIN MACAULEY PUBLISHERS™
LONDON • CAMBRIDGE • NEW YORK • SHARJAH

Copyright © Michoel Levy (2018)

The right of Michoel Levy to be identified as author of this work has been asserted by him in accordance with section 77 and 78 of the Copyright, Designs and Patents Act 1988.

All rights reserved. No part of this publication may be reproduced, stored in a retrieval system, or transmitted in any form or by any means, electronic, mechanical, photocopying, recording, or otherwise, without the prior permission of the publishers.

Any person who commits any unauthorised act in relation to this publication may be liable to criminal prosecution and civil claims for damages.

A CIP catalogue record for this title is available from the British Library.

ISBN 9781528903837 (Paperback)
ISBN 9781528903844 (Hardback)
ISBN 9781528903851 (E-Book)

www.austinmacauley.com

First Published (2018)
Austin Macauley Publishers Ltd
25 Canada Square
Canary Wharf
London
E14 5LQ

If I could tell a tale of fire
To kindle in the night
With words of flame and truth to pierce
The dark's deceit with light

If I could set a ship to sea
With storm winds in its sails
And lightning cast atop the mast
To shine when all hope fails,

Or set an army marching forth
To fight a thousand foes.
I'd set the sky on fire to light
The way to Thunder Rose.

If I could take that storm in hand
A sword in which to trust
The tempest blast within my grasp
I'd shatter death to dust!

And tell a tale to soothe sore hearts
Of ill's despair and scheme.
Poor actors, we, each playing parts
In tales that others dream.

I'd tell a tale of fire to thaw
Cruel winter's bitter snows
A tale that whisp'ring angels speak
I'd tell of Thunder Rose!

Prologue

It is night in the city's marketplace.
Huddling beggars pull tight their scant rags
Against the fingers of night's cold caress.
Crouched in the doorways of the empty shops
They await the rising warmth of morning
To bring hope of a more fortunate day.
Rats nuzzle garbage the beggars have left
With one ear cocked for the stealthy footfall
Of predator puss on her nightly prowl.
Few stars show through the haze and dusty veil
To pierce the all-embracing blanket night.
The only sounds, the tramp of the watchmen,
The rattle of a lantern on a pole
And the whisper of the wind swirling dust.

The market lies in the midst of a town
Upon a road that stretches east and west.
Merchants come upon this road with cargo;
Silk and patterned cloth, perfume, scented oils,
Dyes and spice, the works of each craftsman's art,
Painted vases for the parlours of queens,
Hidden jewels fit for an emperor's crown,
Ironware and tin, all manner of stuff
Is traded here in the town's market place
Where the merchants meet and haggle their price.
They argue, sigh and pull their noses to
Slap their foreheads and sneer in derision
At the shoddy goods on a rival's stall.
They shout and wave, they laugh and shake hands

With another deal done, then turn to look
For new merchandise to pay their way home.

On the road, fortunes are made by the brave
Where Providence alone saves from peril.
The desert and overpowering sea
Have devoured many before journey's end
Saw labour's fruits and the homecoming hearth.

There are other things tucked in the cargo,
Rolled in blankets with documents and deeds,
Nestled tight amongst the phials and jars,
In pouches with rubies, locked in boxes.
Sweeter than perfume, more precious than pearls
Stories are traded too upon this road
And today, a storyteller will come.
But for now, the market is night's domain.

The morning star rises, herald of dawn
And brings the first custom to the town square
Wholesalers who supply the shops and inns
With the produce they need to ply their trade.
They each take off the shutters from their stalls.
This one gives a loaf to an orphan boy
Who spent the night sleeping in his doorway.
The waif eats it there and then slinks away
To find somewhere else to wait and dream
Of comfort, and a mother and a bed.

With the first light, the marching farmers come.
With hoes and goads mounted on their shoulders
They trudge to distant fields to start their work
Whilst in the city, scholars rise from bed
To resume their candlelit devotions.
A housemaid clears ash from her mistress's hearth.
A servant spreads his sleeping master's cloak
Inspecting for dust or for a frayed thread.
Mothers cajole, threaten and offer bribes

To children too reluctant to leave beds
Entered with protest so shortly before.

The artisan sets tools upon his bench
And the factory girl prepares her lunch.
Wrapped in a cloth, she tucks it at her waist.
She leaves and locks the door, then goes to work
To earn an honest wage and dream the day.

Our storyteller comes to the town square,
Surveys a place to sit and set his stool.
None will listen now, but they will see him
Setting out his carpet, flute, drum and harp
And they will tell their friends and make a note
To come later, to sit and listen then.

With patch-coloured clothes and his too-long hat
Great leather boots, his baubles and bells
He sits to tune his harp and strums a chord.
The children dawdling to school see him there
Run excited, each to tell his mother
"A storyteller! A storyteller!
"Can we come? Can we listen after school?"
"If the teacher says that you have been good.
"If he says you have learnt your lessons well
"Then I will buy you an apple to eat
"And you may sit and listen to stories."
And off they run to tell friends and playmates
"Go tell your mother and you can come, too!"

The girls on their way to the factory
Change their lunchtime plans to eat in the square.
Let the world slip humdrum by while they spend
An hour at sail upon his story seas
To a distant and more beautiful land.
But first, there is work. The day must begin.

The storyteller has been seen by all

He breaks night's fast in peaceful privacy
The shadow of a market trader's stall.
And with a flask of water by his side
He sits to await the day's first custom.
Farmers from the hills who return today
Have an hour to spare before going home.
Yesterday they sold a season's produce.
Today they buy for their village supplies
That can only be bought in the city
Here in the market where all things are sold.

He has tales for every ear and purse
Though, in truth, he does not look at day's end
To count the coins lying in his hat.
There is always enough food in his bowl
And he has always slept somehow each night.
Whether the soft bed of a patron's house
Or the wooden cot of a poor man's shack
He has had hospitality from all.
And, yes, he has slept a night out of doors
Beneath the stars or a tree in the rain
Sheltering better his harp than his head.
So he does not examine a man's purse
Before deciding which tale he should tell.
Penniless beggars are welcome to sit
And listen, too, if they do not disturb.
He will be no poorer for their presence.

Morning passes, listeners come and go.
Some request a tale to suit their fancy
Some let him lead wheresoever he will
Till the sun rises to its noontime height.

Now come the factory girls together
To sit with their lunch and make their request.
What tale do they demand? Romance, of course!
"Let us dream, let the princess be pretty.
"Let the knight be strong, bravehearted and true.

"Let him conquer all for his lady love!"
He tells a tale to slake their heartfelt thirst
Till the punctual tyrant chimes its call.

They linger yet, and so gently he says
"You may know my tales are true. Would we cry?
"Would we care, for things that never happened
"To folk who never were?" They smile and rise
Returning, just a little late, to work.

After that, schoolchildren in squirming rows
Poking and pinching while their mothers scold
Till the storyteller tells the mothers
"If you wish to browse in the market place
"The children will be well till you return."
The mothers fall silent and listen, too
As he plays and begins a lively tale.
And with moonbeams in their eyes, they sit still
As children do, to hear his tale unfold.
And when the tale is done, the children ask
"Is your story true?" He winks and tells them
"I never made up a false story yet."
And with that answer they must be content
For it is all the answer that they will get.

The day is turning to cool even time.
The wood sellers arrive with kindling sticks.
The market traders each shutter their stalls.
The townsfolk go one by one to their homes.
Migrant workers take supper in the inns
In a company of travelling folk
All those who make their home upon the road.

Our storyteller removes to the park
To sit beneath a tree and eat his bread.
His day's work is not done. Tales still to tell.
Some stories shy away from light
Some need the warmth and flicker of a fire

Some are told only by starlight's soft glow.
There are flowers that bloom only at night
When the heart is laid bare to love's sweet ache.

And there in the park, he awaits his guests
Singly or in pairs the listeners come
Some bring a blanket to set on damp grass
One brings sticks to make a fire on the stones
Beside where the night's host sits with his harp
One brings a shawl and dainty cakes to share.
She offers one to the storyteller.
He thanks her, smiling, puts it to one side
"For later," then he tunes his harp once more
For the shrinking wood in the cool night air.

He starts to play a soft improvised tune.
His notes swirl with the rising twist of smoke,
Above the crackling twigs and glowing fire
Drifting through branches of the tree above
To where the bats fly out to leave the town
On a curving path to their feeding grounds
In the orchards at the foot of the hills.
A night hawk hovers on currents of air
Searching for its prey, those who leave the path.

The notes of his harp fly with birds and bats
Beyond the town, to scale the mountain slope
Colours once jaded by dull city dust
Are here revealed in the clear mountain air.
Pained cries once stifled by vanity's cares
Tear from the heart to rend mountain rock
And fall as cascades tumbling from the peaks
Till the heart finds solace in the freedom
Of tears that once festered in lone silence.
Laughter, not the caw of the tavern drunk
Nor the poisoned satire of the court wit
Is here the guiltless song of pure heart's joy.

Let us grasp light from the star-rich heavens
We shall not lessen night's jewels thereby.
Our song will sit on mountains as night falls.
Come, hear this tale that comes from the mountains.
This is the story of the Thunder Rose.

Chapter 1

In the mountains that lie between the kingdoms of the East and the kingdoms of the West, there has, from time to time, stood the little kingdom of the passes. It has lasted, sometimes for a century, sometimes longer, sometimes not so long, before being torn apart once again by the rivalries and feuds of the ruling families of its disparate regions. Time and again, it has fallen into the fragmented rule of local powers, and the roads and the passes have become once more the haunt of raiders, bandits and thieves.

One such kingdom was forged by Gilbet. He was, at first, the head of one of the mountain families and became so at an early age, following the untimely passing of his father.

As a youth, he had travelled and had been schooled in foreign lands. Now, as head of his family, with what he had learnt of military strategy and diplomacy, together with his own resources of ruthless and business-like pragmatism, he set about the task of carving a path through the mountains and persuading the leaders of other families that there was more profit to be made in establishing a road that could afford safe passage than there had ever been in banditry.

For ten years, he waged a bloody campaign, forming alliances by persuasion or by force until he had, at last, forged a confederacy that could guarantee the safe passage of a cargo from one side of the mountains to the other.

Gilbet sought to woo speculators with his offer of escort. The merchants, at first, viewed the invitation with distrust and suspicion, but those who dared to take up the offer, found rich rewards. Others soon followed, who preferred to pay duties and taxes for the armed escort of the confederacy army rather than to risk the long and arduous road through the dry deserts of the north or the uncertain perils of the sea and its pirates to the south.

The merchants passing through brought great prosperity, and the leaders of the confederacy consented to appoint Gilbet as their king, at least for now and as long as profits would flourish.

The increased traffic attracted the attention of bandits seeking plunder, but Gilbet's retribution against those who dared assail the caravans was swift and thorough. Gibbets stood on the hilltops above every pass. Any village harbouring bandits was razed to ruins and its inhabitants left to wander the hills. Soon, none dared to molest any merchant who employed the guardians of the new kingdom's roads.

With his new-found wealth, Gilbet established the seat of his power among his people in the town that lay in the heart of his kingdom. The town was in the kingdom's central valley, through which the main mountain road and all the trade would pass. There he built his own gorgeous palace, and there he settled down to raise his family.

Dissent was never far away. Some argued that The King kept too much to himself and held wealth in the central valley away from the common folk of the hills. Others argued that the treatment of bandits was too harsh and that a little banditry was no bad thing to discourage those who sought to avoid the main roads and tolls, and also to remind merchants of the gratitude that they owed for safe passage. Others complained of the foreigners at court whom The King had brought in to assist the growing bureaucracy in the governance of his kingdom.

The King always kept his eye open for treachery and intrigues with spies upon his spies, and he was cautious never to take for granted the negotiable loyalties of those who had not so long before been bandit chiefs yet now assumed titles and honorifics in the fledgling kingdom.

The King and his queen had four children together before a springtime fever took the life of The Queen and left

The King a widower with a young family. He now assumed the role of a father more than of a king, leaving much of the governance of the country to the efficient bureaucracy that he had established.

All his care and precautions ultimately did not avail to protect The King and his family.

One day, he was sitting to take lunch with his two eldest sons, whom he had been grooming for leadership, when the younger arose, clutching his stomach, saying that he felt unwell. He was a very peculiar colour and fell face downward onto the table before him.

Servants rushed to the young man's side while The King called frantically for doctors, but it was already too late. His eyes bulged and he was not breathing. The King and his eldest son stared at each other, both turning pale in the dawning horror that he had been poisoned and that they had each eaten from the same food. How long must they wait before the same fate befell them? With doctors already on the way, The King called out to clear the room, to summon a scribe and to bring his only daughter, Elzbet, without delay. Servants hastened to fulfil The King's commands whilst surgeons tried in vain to elicit signs of life from the fallen prince.

Chapter 2

Elzbet was playing in the palace gardens with her cousins and friends when the urgent call came from the servants to attend her father. The princess turned cold with fear as she ran with them through the palace grounds to the private dining chamber. She arrived there as her eldest brother was being carried out through the antechamber upon a stretcher with his face covered.

When she arrived in the dining room, she saw that it was almost empty. The King sat red and perspiring in a large chair, dictating to a scribe, whilst his personal physician worked quickly and meticulously around him with his lancets, phials and potions. The physician had been instructed that to attempt to save The King's life was most likely futile. He must endeavour to prolong The King's life by whatever means lay at his disposal for so many minutes and seconds as he might to enable The King to give his last instructions to the kingdom and to his daughter, and this the physician laboured faithfully to do.

The King looked up as Elzbet arrived but did not interrupt the flow of his instructions as she knelt before him and he tightly grasped her hand.

The King dictated for the kingdom at large that, following the tragic passing of his two eldest sons, he was appointing his daughter, Elzbet, as his heir. He himself had taken ill and was under strict instructions of his esteemed doctor to rest in solitude, consulting only with those closest to him.

During the period of his illness, Elzbet would act as his regent. As such, she would be acting in The King's name and the kingdom must obey her every word as they would his, and, whilst the kingdom might pray for The King to reign for many more and happy years, upon his passing, they must obey Elzbet as queen as they had always obeyed their king.

The King finished his dictation and the scribe handed the document to him. The king, a man of letters, read the document, signed it with a shaking hand, then handed it to his adviser, Darmid, to seal with The King's signet. He ordered the scribe to leave the room and prepare seventy copies of the document without delay.

Now The King turned to Elzbet, whose hand he took again. His arms were turning red, although his knuckles were white as he spoke and the surgeon fought to turn back the course of the poison that flowed through The King's veins.

He told Elzbet that, whilst her surviving brother might be older, he was appointing her as his heir and that, upon his passing, she would be the monarch. For her sake and for the sake of the kingdom, for her safety and theirs, she must follow his final instructions as closely to the letter as possible.

Firstly, whatever was to happen, she must not permit the announcement of his death until all of the nobles and the heads of all families of power were assembled in the capital and under her control. Secondly, she must seek out and bring to justice those who had committed this treachery, and she should do so without mercy and without delay.

Elzbet listened intently to his every word as he spoke to tell her so much of what he had previously told only to his eldest son.

He said, "I have ruled by fear because I have had to. You will only survive if the kingdom survives, and the kingdom will only survive if you rule with strength, but you must do so with truth. Do not tolerate any injustice. Show mercy when you can, but show no weakness in this!"

The King looked at the seats where his sons had sat but half an hour before and he said, "Kill the men who killed my sons. Kill them." He began to weep as he said his sons' names over and over until suddenly, his grip tightened, his body convulsed and the life left him.

Elzbet released her father's motionless hand. The room was silent, empty, save for the body of The King, Elzbet, the surgeon, the captain of The King's guard and The King's old and trusted friend and advisor, Darmid.

Numb with shock, Elzbet stared, as the surgeon and the captain laid her father's body on the cold stone flags. Darmid closed The King's eyes and covered his face with a cloak. The captain closed the windows and shutters, and the surgeon said that if The King's body was to remain with them in the room, then the room should be kept cold. Elzbet was able to nod, and the surgeon poured a jug of water onto the logs in the hearth to douse the fire.

Instinctively and to preserve herself from panic, Elzbet busied herself with preparing to carry out her father's last instructions. She placed four chairs around the table, and sat at the table's head. Darmid, the captain and the surgeon sat with her, and Elzbet asked what had been done to fulfil her father's last command. The captain replied that he had already despatched men to search the kitchens, storehouses and throughout the palace. He had given orders that the city's gates be closed, that soldiers be posted to all roads out of the city and that the entire Royal Guard be placed on alert.

They agreed between them that The King's body would remain in the inner chamber, and that Elzbet, Darmid and the surgeon would stay there too. Only the captain would sit in the antechamber. From there, he would take out orders and bring in reports or whatever else might be required.

As soon as the first copies of The King's letter returned, Elzbet worked with Darmid to check and to seal each one. Each letter was sent with a troop of men to be delivered to the nobles and to be promulgated throughout the kingdom. The same troops as would deliver The King's letter would be responsible for bringing in the nobles of each family and region under guard to the palace.

No one stood upon their honour or upon ceremony as they worked tirelessly to ensure that The King's final orders were put into effect. The captain ran back and forth through the vacant outer chamber, bringing in news as it was received and taking out orders to those who waited upon The King's word or at least upon that of his regent. He brought in papers with reports and took out sealed replies. He passed out orders for refreshments and brought in cups of drink and plates of food.

The surgeon's task was to preserve the dignity of the body of The King and to make its presence tolerable whilst maintaining the appearance that The King still lived. He sent orders with the captain for oils, medicaments and healing foods in The King's name, as well as the tools and lotions that the physician would need to stave off decay.

The country was instructed by a sealed letter from Elzbet as regent to pray for her father's recovery and health, and the surgeon announced that The King's condition was at least stable.

Chapter 3

Within a few hours, word arrived that the first nobles had arrived in carriages at the palace, those who had residences in the city or estates in the nearby hills and valleys. Each one was to be taken to his own designated room in the palace without opportunity for communication. A servant would be appointed from the royal household to attend to his needs and requests, and to bring such possessions as one might reasonably require, but apart from that, none was to have contact with any other. They would be housed in comfort and dignity in royal apartments but under close guard at all times.

As the hours passed, news came in that two men had been seen fleeing from the city and had been pursued and captured with evidence of their close involvement in the treason.

By evening, information arrived from the troops that had been despatched to the country that there had been attacks on garrisons on the roads and rebellion was brewing. Three battalions of men had been encountered in separate locations, each within half a day's march of the city, assembled and waiting seemingly for news of The King's death. Two of the three armies had disbanded and fled to the hills as soon as they heard that The King still lived, but the third and largest had maintained ranks and still stood poised and ready to march.

As night fell, the captain issued a summons to all men able to bear arms. They were to answer the muster at dawn in a field by the city gates to be ready to march with sword, spear and armour. Criers went through the dark city streets to issue the call to arms and to announce that those who would not answer the muster would be deemed traitors. None who were in health refused the call.

Through the night, Elzbet, Darmid and the captain drafted a letter in The King's name and in The King's manner to be read to the troops at dawn before they marched. The letter announced that The King greatly regretted that he would not march at the head of his men at this time as he had so often in the past, that he was, at once, humbled and made proud by the love and loyalty of his subjects that they showed in drawing together to avenge the attack on their king and the murder of the country's princes. Only by such unity of purpose and such brotherhood would the country be spared from the ravages and devastation of civil war.

Lastly, The King looked forward to his return to health and the day when he would rejoice together with his people in their success in preserving the peace and prosperity of the nation.

The captain sent out his lieutenant to deliver and read the letter to the troops whilst he himself remained by the dead king with The Queen, Darmid and the surgeon.

On a damp and misty autumn morning, the army assembled and began its march. Those who, a day before, had been farmers, tailors and shopkeepers, were now soldiers marching to avenge and to protect their kingdom.

Heralds went ahead with trumpets to announce in every village square along the way that any village that was found to have supported the rebellion or from where a man was found to have come to join the rebel forces would, following the quelling of the rebellion, be razed to the ground without exception. The King would extend mercy to all who remained loyal but would visit swift vengeance on those who did not.

Scouts were sent ahead and returned to the marching army to say that ten thousand men of one of the country's largest and most populous region were gathered in a valley, waiting. The army that marched numbered more than double that.

Those commanding the march were ordered to slow their progress and to delay their arrival. Rumours spread that The King, in his mercy, wished to afford opportunity to the rebel forces to surrender or flee. Others said that The King wished to have time to overtake and join them in exacting vengeance.

By the time the force arrived, the rebel camp was in disarray. The men had fled to the mountains. No stragglers remained and their leaders were found bound and ready to be delivered to The King's men under the guard of men of their own ranks beneath a flag of truce. No sword had been unsheathed. No arrow had been loosed. Not a drop of blood was spilt.

Meanwhile in the city, carriages were arriving by the hour, bringing the nobles to the palace. Soldiers conducted the occupants of the carriages to their lavish prisons. Some of those arriving were compliant, respecting the urgency of the hour. Others were surly and sullen, protesting the sleight to their honour and at being deprived of their liberty, their servants and their sleep.

Shortly after nightfall, the messengers from the field reached the city, proclaiming the success of the campaign and celebrating that there had been no fighting at all. The city cheered the news, and the families of those who had marched rejoiced in the knowledge that their husbands and fathers were safe and alive, yet still, the city remained alert.

The men who had been arrested confessed their guilt under questioning and named their paymasters as the heads of the regions that had raised forces for the rebellion.

Many of the remaining nobles arrived through the night, dishevelled and bad tempered after travelling on the uneven mountain roads through hours that they would sooner have spent in a warm and soft bed.

The most immediate crisis had passed, but still, Elzbet, Darmid and the captain did not sleep. Only the physician, whose work was less than the others, took time to lie down and to rest.

Chapter 4

It was shortly after noon on the following day. Elzbet and her trio of advisers, all those who had remained by the body of The King, agreed that the time had come to announce The King's death. The heads of all but the most distant regions were accounted, whether in the palace already or known to be in transit, and those remaining were of too little power or influence to pose any threat

They sat in the cold room at a table littered with the bread that remained of the most recent meal they had taken. The Queen sat with a shawl over her shoulders and reviewed a list that had recently arrived of the names of those known or suspected to have been involved in the assassination and revolt.

The names of the chief conspirator and his family were well known to Elzbet. He was a man who had been close to The King from his earliest years and campaigns, and the two families had grown up together. Now greed and ambition had overcome friendship, and he had turned rebel, traitor and murderer.

Elzbet read down the list of names. "Were all of his sons involved?" she asked the captain.

"Perhaps not all," the captain replied. "His youngest son is an officer of the Royal Guard and was on duty at the time of the attack. We do not have evidence of his involvement, but we have arrested him out of caution."

The captain continued, "Your Majesty may feel it appropriate to adopt a root-and-branch approach. He will be disenfranchised. He may harbour resentment, and if Your Majesty does not take action to deal with him now, he could form a rallying point for any future attempt at rebellion." The captain concluded cautiously, "He would be the last shoot of a poisoned vine, and I believe that your father would have adopted such a course."

Elzbet considered the captain's words and said, "I am not my father. I am a queen, and not a tyrant. I will not execute a man without evidence of a crime."

The captain shifted in his chair. "Your Majesty may live to regret the decision," he said uneasily.

"And you will be there to say you told me so," Elzbet said quite firmly, and with that, she stood and announced that she was going to bed.

The surgeon looked up from the couch where he lay and asked would The Queen like anything to help her to sleep. It had been more than two days since Elzbet had seen her bed or had rested. Elzbet said that she would not need anything.

She had become so accustomed to the presence of her father's body in the room, that it seemed quite natural for her to say "Goodnight, Daddy" before she left. In the two days since his death, she had not shed a single tear for her father. There had not been the time.

Chapter 5

Elzbet slept for a few hours and rose in the late afternoon. By that time, the palace and country were officially in mourning and she was the ruling monarch. The servants no longer addressed her as "Your Highness", but as "Your Majesty". All of the staff hurried about their business quietly and when they spoke, they spoke in hushed tones.

Although the threat of civil war appeared to have passed, there was still an air of nervousness in the kingdom. The people had known all of The King's sons. The two eldest had been recognised as capable and responsible young men, worthy of leadership and commanding respect. The surviving brother, at eighteen years of age and two years Elzbet's senior, was also known, although considered to be flighty, immature, rather too fond of pranks and parties; a juvenile with a taste for pleasures.

Little, however, was known about Elzbet outside the circle of her intimates. The King had always kept her guarded, away from the public eye.

Following the death of his wife, The King had appointed a governess for his daughter who, he hoped, would not spoil or indulge her inasmuch as this was possible with a king's only daughter.

The King had appointed teachers upon whom he could rely for their discretion as much as for their knowledge and had found classmates whose parents The King felt he could trust.

Elzbet was reputed to be a kind child, quiet in company, caring and considerate with her friends. It was known that she had a sense of humour and that she had been the apple of her father's eye. Save for that, little was known.

Now that she was formally queen and not regent, her first official duty would be to pass judgement on the men who had murdered her father and brothers. She sat upon a throne in the courtroom accompanied by justices and clerks as the two men were led before her in chains. There was no evidence to hear. The men had admitted their guilt and the facts were confirmed. Their faces were sallow and drawn. They were bruised and they limped when they walked.

Elzbet looked at them coldly and they elicited no emotion from her. They were base and worthless creatures, an affront to human dignity who had sold all vestiges of compassion for a purse of money.

She spoke dispassionately as she passed sentence. She informed the men that they would be executed in public on the morrow and any property they owned would be forfeit to the crown. She told them, "As you have confessed your guilt, your widows will not be left penniless. They will be brought here to work for me. I will find husbands for them in due time so that they will be spared the ignominy of having to beg, and your children will have step-fathers who will feed them. As an orphan myself, I have pity on orphans."

The men stood silent with their heads bowed. They murmured their thanks to The Queen for her mercies and were led away to await their fate.

Elzbet spent part of the afternoon arranging with her household the schedule for the coming days. The funerals of her father and brothers would take place a day after the executions. That way, her father could be laid to rest in peace. It would also afford time to Elzbet's sole remaining brother to return from school abroad. Even with swift horses, he would not arrive earlier than in two days. She did not want to delay the funerals any later than that.

Execution would be carried out on the conspirators on the same day as those who had carried out the murders. There were three leaders of the conspiracy, being the heads of the three families that had raised armies. Several of their underlings were still under investigation to ascertain in each case their involvement and the degree of their compliance, and no doubt, further trials and executions would follow.

The country's nobles were now all under guard and would remain so until the executions. In the morning, each one would be brought to The Queen separately to swear oaths of allegiance. Each would be brought alone, would swear and leave before the next would enter. Once they had all sworn, they would be released to attend the executions, although the palace would still offer its hospitality if they so required.

None would be forced to swear, but for those who did not wish to swear in the morning, there was still space on the scaffold that afternoon.

The executions were to take place in public in the great courtyard to the fore of the palace. Carpenters were even now assembling the scaffold with seating for The Queen and the attendant nobility.

With all in place and preparations underway, Elzbet retired to her bed early, this time accepting the physician's offer of a soothing drink to afford her a full night's sleep. She would be rising early in the morning to begin the task of hearing the oaths of those who would be her ministers and regional governors.

In the morning, she sat in the throne room to receive her visitors. They entered through one door, swore allegiance and left through another. Some expressed condolences for The Queen's tragic loss. Some added a few words of a fond memory of something her father had said, a kindness done for them or for another in an hour of need. A few added their own words to wish that The Queen should enjoy a long and happy reign, free of strife and sadness. Most, however, presented themselves formally and curtly, limiting their words to the text of the oath alone. Although all seemed uneasy swearing allegiance to the young queen, none declined to swear while outside the crowd were gathering to await the executions.

The oath-taking ceremonies, whilst brief and efficiently managed, occupied the entire morning. When the ceremonies had finished, sixty-seven in all, as the leaders of the rebelling regions awaited their fate that afternoon and were not amongst them, Elzbet allowed herself a short respite to take lunch. Following the physician's advice, she ate little.

As she sat taking her meal in a small, private room above the courtyard, she could hear the gathered crowd begin to boo and jeer. They had been assembling since the early morning, and now while their queen ate, the murderers of their king were being led out before them to the scaffold. Elzbet took no interest and did not look up to see as, for several minutes, the noise of the booing grew louder and louder until it reached its climax in a great cheer, signalling that the executioners had fulfilled their task and justice had been done.

It was now the turn of the conspirators, and this, at least, Elzbet would need to attend in person.

A lady-in-waiting sat in attendance by the door as her sole maid while she ate in silence. A bell rang and Elzbet looked up. The maid stood and opened the door. She spoke to one outside and then turned to announce to The Queen that they were ready and waiting for her downstairs. Elzbet took a last sip of water, wiped her mouth and stood.

The sounds from the courtyard had died down somewhat. Elzbet still did not look out of the window as she passed. She had no desire to see the tasks of clearing up while the executioners prepared for her arrival.

She had chosen to wear a sober brown and black gown for the occasion of her first public appearance as queen. She would not don her formal mourning clothes until after the funeral.

Outside the room where she had dined, there was a landing and a flight of stairs that led down to a large high-ceilinged hallway. There in the hallway, the company that would escort her were waiting. Darmid would stand at her side and they would be followed by several of the senior ministers and an honour guard of twenty soldiers.

Elzbet left the maid standing at the top of the stairs as she went down to take her place at the head of the entourage behind the great doors that led to the courtyard. The doors were several times the height of a man and wide enough for two teams of horses to stand side by side.

As she took her place, the guard formed orderly rows behind.

"How are you?" asked Darmid as they waited for the doors to open.

"I am well," said Elzbet pleasantly. "If I faint, perhaps you can tell everyone that I have not had enough sleep over the past few nights."

The rising excited hubbub of the crowd outside mixed to a cacophony with the scream of the nerves in her ears until all sounded like the braying of a pack of hounds.

A soldier looked through a latticed hatch in the door to see that all was ready outside for The Queen's arrival and then turned to inform the waiting group. The Queen nodded and two guards opened the great high doors.

Sunlight streamed in as the doors opened and The Queen stepped forward. The crowd fell silent and doffed their hats at her appearance and out of respect for her mourning. She walked between them along a raised wooden walkway a foot or so above the cobbles. Her entourage followed behind and she met the eyes of no one as she walked.

The nobles were standing waiting in three rows by tiered seats on the viewing stand of the scaffold. There was a padded chair for The Queen and room for her entourage to stand at her side. Three blocks and baskets were set before the chair with empty coffins on the ground below. The platform was still wet from having been freshly mopped and the executioners stood with their axes and tools at their side.

Elzbet came to her chair, sat down and the nobles sat. The crowd was silent but Elzbet's head still howled.

At the far end of the courtyard, a guard opened a door and drums began to roll. Soldiers led out three men in leather hoods, with chains upon them. Their clothes, once so fine, were tattered and stained.

At once, the crowd began again to jeer, shouting their indignation and derision at the prisoners, heedless of the presence of The Queen. Two of the men walked by their own strength, their heads bowed within their hoods. The legs of the third quivered and gave way beneath him as he was forced to walk, and so the soldiers half-carried him, squirming and quivering, whimpering uncontrollably as they pulled him along. The people screamed and cursed, they hissed, spat at them and tried to strike them as they passed.

The nobles watched in silence. They all knew the men who were being led to their deaths. Some amongst the assembled nobles had been the condemned men's friends. But today, no one called them friend.

The men were led up to the platform before The Queen. There, the hoods of all three were removed to show the condemned men's faces to The Queen and to the furious throng. Two were grey and lifeless as stone. The third was white and trembling with fear. His eyes bulged as he stared from The Queen to the block, basket and waiting coffin, and his mouth frothed around his gag. Whereas the men she had seen the previous day had left her feeling cold and unmoved, these men aroused only revulsion. Two were known to be men of greedy ambition. Their leader was a man whom The King had befriended and trusted. The whimpering one was an easily led fop with a low reputation, having a taste for drinking parties and gaming. They had all once been no more than petty tribal chieftains, hearing the squabbles of mountain villagers. They had become the wealthy lords of a prosperous realm due to the successes of her father.

Elzbet had seen enough and motioned with her hand to order that the hoods be replaced, scarcely masking her impatience for the job to be completed. Once the hoods were replaced, the men were manhandled and made to kneel at their blocks sideways to The Queen so that their backs should not be disrespectfully towards her, nor should their blood stain her dress.

The condemned men were in place and the drums began to roll again. The officer supervising raised his hand, the executioners raised their axes and the howling of the crowd rose in pitch. Elzbet looked to a stray thread that she pulled from the arm of her chair as the officer dropped his hand, the axes fell and the howling fell silent. Two cut cleanly through, but the third axeman called for his victim to be held for him to fetch another blow. Soldiers tried to hold the man still and the executioner called for ropes. He was embarrassed and apologising to The Queen for the delay as they bound the struggling man and held tightly to the ropes to hold him in place. Two more strokes were required before the task was complete and now the executioners could hold up their gory trophies for the delighted crowd to see.

As soon as she heard the cheers, The Queen rose to leave the platform, returning with her entourage, walking quickly along the wooden walkway amidst the clapping, shouting and whistling of the cheering crowd.

She had comported herself with cool restraint and dignity throughout. Once inside and with the doors securely closed, Darmid turned to congratulate The Queen on her conduct, but The Queen had already disappeared from sight.

Chapter 6

Elzbet kept her own company for much of the rest of the day, sitting in her father's room in the private royal apartments. The servants who had been busy with putting away his personal belongings left her to be by herself while they found other things to occupy them.

In the evening, Elzbet went to her own room, where the servants were packing. She had chosen to delay taking up residence in her father's room until a week or so after the funeral as a respect to her father. Nonetheless, preparations for the move were already underway.

Her own possessions were surprisingly few. She had her dresses, several of which she had outgrown but not yet discarded and others of which were unsuitable for her new station. There were her bedroom ornaments, her mother's jewellery, her brushes and her mirror.

Then there was her dolls house. It had been a gift from the guilds of the city to The King and his queen on the occasion of the birth of their daughter. The master carpenters had fashioned the house. The guild of cabinet makers had made the furniture, the beds, wardrobes and dressers. The potters' guild had made the crockery while the knifesmiths had made the cutlery and kitchen implements. The guild of toymakers had made the wooden dolls and toys for the nursery. The King's own tailor had made the robes for the master of the house and the royal dressmaker had made dresses for the mistress. On the wall of the parlour hung two cameo portraits, one of The King and one of his queen, painted in miniature by the royal portrait painter. The table on which the house stood formed a paved courtyard on which stood a beautiful carriage with footmen and two fine horses, one sable, one grey.

The move was overseen by Lady Harkett. Until recently, she had been Elzbet's governess and was now appointed as her senior lady-in-waiting. She saw Elzbet standing by the dolls house, looking at the paintings in the parlour, and walked over to stand by The Queen's side.

"Do you remember your mother?" asked Lady Harkett gently.

"A little," said Elzbet, then after a pause, asked, "Was my mother beautiful?"

"I thought so," said Lady Harkett.

"And what did other people think?" asked Elzbet.

"They also thought so," said Lady Harkett, then she said, "But I especially thought so."

Elzbet looked wistfully at the dolls house and asked, "Will I be able to take my dolls house with me?"

Lady Harkett paused and said, "I do not think that your dolls house would be suitable for the royal apartments."

"I thought as queen I could do whatever I wanted," said Elzbet pointedly.

Lady Harkett replied, "That is a princess, not a queen."

***

Elzbet was still asleep when her brother, Calum, arrived at the palace shortly after dawn the next day. He had ridden partly through the night and had slept little to be sure to be on time for his father's and brothers' funeral.

When Elzbet awoke, she was told of her brother's arrival. She dressed quickly and came down to greet him. They did not say a word as they embraced and wept on each other's shoulders, the only surviving members of their family.

At last, they sat down at a table, holding hands to comfort each other. Elzbet asked Calum how he was and asked about his studies. Even from his small talk, it was clear that he had matured since she last saw him. He was enjoying his studies and spoke admiringly of his teachers.

They spoke briefly about their father's decision to appoint Elzbet as his heir. Calum said that if that was their father's decision, then he was happy not to have the burden of rulership of the kingdom on his young shoulders, and that was the end of the discussion.

Calum was to represent the family at the funeral, leaving Elzbet free to say her quiet and tearful farewells from the privacy of the palace before the funeral procession left to go through the town to the burial ground.

Later that morning, the procession left the palace gates promptly. The coffins were borne on three black hearses and Calum walked slowly behind. The cortege passed through the main roads of the town and the townsfolk walked behind in silent respect, many following all the way to the burial ground on the hillside above the city. All was conducted with solemn dignity before Calum returned from the ceremony to sit by his sister, to receive condolences and to begin their mourning.

Chapter 7

The Queen's new officers announced on her behalf that she would deliver her maiden address to the nobles, ministers and officials a week after the funeral. Calum had originally intended to stay long enough to hear his sister's first speech but changed his plans to leave a day earlier, on the morning of the day of the speech. He had already received one anonymous note which said simply, 'You have supporters.' And he had no wish to receive any more.

During the address, The Queen would announce the date of her coronation. Her counsellors advised her to fix a date as soon as possible to consolidate her position, to take advantage of the wave of national unity to confirm her hold upon the throne. Certainly, she should delay no longer than the end of the month, her counsellors advised.

Not for the last time, Elzbet heard but did not take the advice that was offered.

Elzbet had no experience of public speaking and her advisers were concerned that her voice might not carry in the great stone hall. They consulted an architect who advised that matters might be improved by hanging heavy drapes on the walls. The advisers arranged this and asked The Queen if she might yet require an announcer to relay her words when she spoke, but Elzbet replied, "If men strain their ears for whispered slanders, they can fall still to hear their queen's soft speech. If I have something worthy of being said, I can say it quietly and they will be sure to hear. If what I have to say is not worth saying, then it matters little if they hear it or not."

In her address to the nobles, The Queen announced that her coronation would take place the following summer, almost a year away. She said that she wished to have time to mourn properly for her father and brothers and that she wished to allow the country to do the same.

The coronation, she announced, would be celebrated by a great fair, and for that purpose, the town square would be enlarged and improved. It would be renamed 'Coronation Square'. Tenders would be invited straight away for contracts for the improvements and other civil works besides.

Representatives of the monarchies of neighbouring countries would be invited to attend the fair and coronation, and the interim would afford opportunity to improve the roads to facilitate their attendance, to shorten their way and to make the travelling more comfortable.

As she announced the plans, those in attendance smiled and smirked one to another. They whispered, "If the little princess wants to spend all her daddy's money on a fashion parade for her friends, then let her do so." It would be all the easier, they said, to step in once the money ran out to rescue the country from The Queen's profligacy. And if, in the meantime, the roads were improved at her expense, that would hurt nobody.

All agreed, however, that for the time being at least, The Queen had bought herself a period of peace, and they could sit back and wait for the invitations to the coronation and fair to arrive.

Chapter 8

Invitations to the coronation were sent to the neighbouring kingdoms and information about the fair was delivered to all of the prominent merchants of the surrounding regions. The proposed civil works and improvements were announced and contractors were invited to submit their proposals and designs and to tender for the work.

A tax of men to provide workers on the roads was imposed upon the hill tribes that had joined the rebellion. They were set to work straight away, widening the roads leading into the city and clearing woodland to the sides of the road to improve security for travellers.

The first responses to invitations that arrived at the palace offices were from the neighbouring monarchies. Their rulers extended their condolences to The Queen and expressed their wishes for her long and peaceful reign. They would be delighted to send their ambassadors and emissaries to attend the coronation on their behalf.

The next to arrive, and not too long afterwards, were the responses from the foreign merchants, saying that they would be attending the fair. Many of the letters of response were delivered by agents of the merchants who, having given their master's response, stayed in the city to arrange accommodation and to inspect the facilities that might be available, as well as the plans for development of the square.

The innkeepers of the larger inns soon realised that they would be able to charge a premium for their best rooms during the fair, but however much they negotiated and demanded, it seemed that the agents were still willing to pay. More agents were arriving by the day from further and further afield, seeking rooms, and more and more bookings were taken.

It was becoming apparent that there were not going to be enough rooms in the existing inns.

Enterprising individuals hurried to offer their services to the visiting agents to find them accommodation and to offer their services to householders in the city to find them paying guests. The entrepreneurs would contract builders on the householders' behalf to enlarge their homes to be used as inns. They promised the householders that however much they would spend on improvements now, they would receive in rent in a single week of the fair, with profits besides.

As the demand for building work increased, men began to arrive from the hills. Anyone who could be spared from the farms came seeking work. All found work and still more workers were needed.

Designs for the bridges and plans for the roads were submitted, judged and approved. Contracts were drafted and signed, and work was commenced. The plans for Coronation Square were amended, enlarged and amended again, now with a grand memorial fountain in the middle of the square in memory of the late king.

Bidding began for the merchants' stalls in the prime locations and the closing date for bids was pushed back to give opportunity to merchants from further afield to arrive. The only subject on anyone's lips was the preparations as it became more and more clear that the great coronation fair was set to be the trade event of the century and no merchant, trader, speculator or investor of substance from a thousand miles around was going to miss it.

Royal families sent new responses to say that they would now be sending royal delegations and might they respectfully request that suitable and appropriate accommodation be arranged. Nobles with mansions in the city vied for the honour of hosting the royal visitors.

Work began on a wide and sturdy bridge to span the great northern river to shorten a merchant train's journey to the capital by more than two days.

Regional governors competed for franchises for inns, tolls and markets along the main trade routes. The successful applicant for each franchise would be the one who could best ensure safety for travellers on the stretch of road that he would maintain.

Throughout the winter, every room of every inn was filled with the newly arrived building crews from the country. Work started early each morning and continued as long as there was light. In the evenings, the taverns rang with the noise of the thirsty builders, whilst nervous contractors offered landlords bribes to close their bars early so that workers might arrive sober and in time to begin their work the next day.

A closing date was fixed for bids for the merchants' stalls and when the date arrived and the stalls were allocated, the agents returned, at last, to their masters, and the city counted the days till the fair would begin.

Spring was late in coming and teams of workers cleared snow from the high roads and passes for construction to recommence. New staging posts were established for a postal service and soldiers patrolled the roads.

All the while, messengers came to and from the palace offices in an endless stream, but The Queen herself was rarely seen.

As summer approached, rumours came of caravans from afar, the like of which had never been seen. Tales of wondrous cargo from the east grew with each telling.

As the day grew yet nearer, the scaffolding came down from buildings and the city could barely be recognised. The last coats of paint were not even dry when the first trains of mules began to arrive.

The fair was about to begin.

Chapter 9

The coronation fair was a tremendous success. From the grand opening by Prince Calum, to the fireworks on the final night, every detail spoke of the meticulous care in preparation.

Even before the fair was formally opened, the streets bustled with trade. Merchandise from the farthest corners of the world filled the stalls. By day, sales were made over the counters and by night, over the tables in the crowded inns and taverns.

Each day, there was scarcely room to move in the square and surrounding roads. Soldiers kept order in the markets and kept traffic moving on the roads into and out of the city. Judges and courts were convened near the markets with weights and measures to settle all disputes.

A grand circus tent for performers was erected in a field outside the city. Singers, bands of musicians, players, jugglers, tumblers, horse riders and clowns took their turns while their managers and agents fixed tours and took bookings for the year ahead.

In the evenings, the smells of roasting meats and pungent, exotic spices filled the air while barrels of wine and beer trundled on wagons through the street.

The innkeepers worked late and woke their bleary-eyed staff early. There was no time to slack. Profits for the year would be made in a few days, and when the fair was gone, it was gone.

At dawn each day, the street cleaners began their work. There was scant time to sweep and wash the cobbles before the bustling trade began again.

At noon on the last day, a great bell was rung and work began to dismantle the stalls and clear the square for the coronation parade. An army of street cleaners cleared away litter whilst others put up flags, bunting and baskets of flowers. There would be fireworks that night, but the fair was over.

In the night, folk stood on the hills and walls around the city to see the fireworks, and by morning, there was no sign that there had been a fair there at all. Crowds of people who had camped out in the street that night lined the way along the side of Coronation Square. Men stood in their laundered tunics and women in their bonnets. Scrubbed children sat at the front, waiting for the parade to begin. Cartloads of cakes and confections arrived from the palace kitchen to be distributed amongst the children. The fair was finished, but the coronation had arrived.

The players and performers entertained the crowd before members of the military band in their dress uniform took their positions on the bandstand. At the appointed hour, the band began to play and the parade began.

The town's guildsmen marched first. Bakers and pastry cooks in spotless starched white, carpenters and masons in their leather aprons, tailors and cobblers each in their dress uniforms and with the tools and badges of their trade marched proudly in their ranks across the square to the beat of the martial band. At the gate of the palace, each of the chosen delegates entered to take his position of honour as the next group arrived.

After the guildsmen came a troop from each of the country's regions under their banners and wearing their family's colours and emblems. Every new group brought a good-natured cheer from the flag-waving crowd.

After that followed the soldiers of the national army with swords at their sides. Then the visiting royal guests and ambassadors rode in grand carriages pulled by brushed and tasselled horses to the palace gates. Their carriages entered to bring the royal visitors to their seats for the ceremony.

Next came the elite Royal Guard in ordered and disciplined mounted ranks. In their black livery and shining helmets, they rode and took their places on duty around the palace walls.

Now after all had marched, there was a hush. A great fanfare blew, trumpets echoing trumpets. Children ran along the side of the square with streamers. Flags were unfurled and a tingle of excitement ran through the crowd.

Drawn by six magnificent white horses, the golden carriage appeared. A cry went up, "Long live The Queen! Long live The Queen!" The Queen was coming. The children sang their coronation song whilst the crowd cheered and chanted.

Elzbet sat in the open carriage with Lady Harkett as her companion. Elzbet had been instructed on how she should conduct herself. She was to hold herself with dignity and poise. If she felt that she must wave, she should not wave to anyone in particular but only to the crowd in general and she should cast her eyes always forward as if gazing to a great and glorious future.

What she actually did was to turn from side to side and wave as excited as any schoolgirl seeing all of her friends at once for the first time in a year. Every child there felt as if The Queen looked and waved directly to him or her alone. Lady Harkett could only sit and sigh at the conduct of her incorrigible erstwhile charge.

At one point on her journey across the square, Elzbet called a sudden halt to the driver of the carriage. A little boy was looking frantically around to find something. The Queen stood and waved to catch the eye of a soldier standing stiffly nearby with a staff and pennant. She mouthed to the soldier as clearly as she could, "He's lost his flag!" pointing urgently to the little boy. She gestured to the soldier to help the boy find it.

The carriage waited while the soldier and others in the crowd searched as best they could, and when none could find the lost flag, the soldier held up his hand in despair and to question what he might do next. "Then give him yours!"

laughed The Queen. The soldier stood to attention, turned and marched formally over, ceremoniously handed his staff and pennant to the pink-eared boy and admonished, "Look after this one or we are both in trouble." And The Queen sat down and gave the order that the driver might now continue.

The crowd continued cheering and Lady Harkett shook her head until Elzbet took her hand and told her that she absolutely must join in the waving on pain of something horrendous she had not even thought of yet, as this was likely to be the last coronation that either of them would ever attend. Elzbet reassured Lady Harkett, "If you are worried that The Queen will be late for her own coronation, you are not to worry. They would not dare start without me."

Lady Harkett started to wave as well in a dignified manner that she hoped would at least set some sort of example for The Queen to follow.

The carriage entered the palace gates. Six maids in silk dresses came to take The Queen's train and to escort her on her ascent to the waiting throne. The nobles in their ceremonial finery, the dignitaries and royal guests all stood while the solemn and majestic music played to accompany The Queen.

Of all the jewels that had been seen that week, none sparkled so brightly, nor caught the eye, as the young queen herself; beautiful yet demure, orphaned and eligible, and, with the success of the coronation fair, the queen of a country that stood at the crossroads of the world's most valuable trade route. The queens and duchesses in attendance looked at their princes, looked back to Elzbet and made their calculations.

Chapter 10

The fair was over and the visitors prepared to leave. The pack animals in the fields outside the city were laden with the purchased merchandise. The merchants shook hands and agreed to meet each other again at next year's fair, for whilst no fair had been announced as yet, all agreed that there must be one. One by one, the caravans and mule trains filed out of the city to begin their long journeys home.

Only a few weeks had passed before the first letters arrived at the palace with suggestions of a possible match for The Queen with references and notes of recommendation praising the qualities of the gentleman concerned. The letters were received and invitations extended in each case for the young man to attend at the palace to meet The Queen.

They came on horseback or in carriages with their attendants and escorts, and each one came bearing gifts. They were all received politely and their gifts graciously accepted, but each one rode away disappointed following his meeting, with a formal letter arriving shortly afterwards to say that, whilst The Queen wished her suitor much happiness for the future, this match was not for her.

The courtiers and townsfolk gossiped and spoke about what The Queen might seek in a husband. Would she marry a powerful ally to lend external support against an internal threat? Would that compromise the country's autonomy? Would she marry for wealth to promote financial stability? Some suggested that The Queen might even marry for love, but all agreed that there was no hurry to decide and that The Queen could choose at her leisure.

Suggestions came from further afield. This one was the son of a fabulously wealthy merchant. This one had a brilliant military career, but none found any more success than the earlier suitors had.

Still the people gossiped, surmised and speculated. Some asserted that The Queen was looking for a man like her father, and where would she find such a one? Others said that perhaps she feared to marry, remembering only too well the fate that had befallen her father and brothers.

The seasons turned. The summer fairs came and came 'round again. The seasons turned to years. The city bustled and the kingdom flourished, yet still, The Queen remained unmarried and alone.

One day, The Queen was sitting at a celebratory meal in honour of the Royal Guard when one of her ministers, perhaps encouraged by the quality of the wine that had been served, ventured to ask, as many often had, what man, if any, The Queen might deign to marry.

"What sort of man would want to marry me?" said The Queen.

"But, Your Majesty," replied the minister, "there are many who would."

"That is as may be," said The Queen, "but I did not enquire as to the number, but the quality. For a man to want to marry me, he would have to be greedy or mad or mad with greed, and neither folly, nor avarice, is a virtue that I seek."

"But Your Majesty does not give them a chance," persisted the minister. "What about the one of whom Your Majesty said she did not like the way that he looked?"

"My dear Lord Chancellor," said The Queen in solemn rebuke, "if you are to quote my words at all, have the grace to quote all of my words. I said that I did not like the way that he looked at me, the way that he looked at my maidservant and the way that he looked at every female that stumbled beneath his gaze."

Those assembled at the table laughed, but the minister continued nonetheless.

"But then there was that poor fellow whose only crime was to ask if you were to marry him, how would you respond to your first argument? Your Majesty replied that you had no way of knowing, as nobody ever had argued with you ever since you had adopted a policy of executing any who did. The poor young man ran from the palace so fast, he arrived home half a day before his horse!"

Again, there was laughter, but The Queen replied innocently, "He had no sense of humour. You can hardly expect me to marry a man with no sense of humour."

The minister was not finished. "There must be one," he said. "Some flower that would win Your Majesty's heart. 'What sun would melt these mountain snows? And when will bloom this maiden rose?'"

Those at the table fell into a nervous silence as they waited to see how The Queen would react. The song *Maiden Rose* was a popular ballad in the taverns of the town, and whilst those who knew The Queen well said that she found the words not unflattering, none had dared yet to recite them publicly in her presence.

The Queen broke the silence to respond patiently. She said, "There is but one, and that is nothing less than a thunder rose." She held up her right hand and said, "And without a thunder rose in this hand, I shall not marry!"

All those around her laughed as one and heartily, too.

The thunder rose was a legend. "The rose that grows where lighting strikes." A thing of rare beauty that if not plucked there and then, would fade and be lost as soon as its thunder had passed from the sky.

It was said that whoever possessed such a treasure, possessed a great gift, but one that came with a great price, for whosoever would prick their flesh with the thorns of the thunder rose would be granted their heart's most true desire, but the cost of that gift would be their very life.

The laughter died down. The minister wiped the tears of mirth from his eyes and the next dishes were brought to the diners as the banquet continued in fine good spirit.

There was one man there who did not laugh when the others laughed. His name was Guylin and he was the sole surviving son of the man who, years before, had led the conspiracy against the old king.

He had remained as a soldier and officer in the Royal Guard ever since. He had never been promoted since that day and typically he would be assigned to posts far away from the palace. On this occasion, however, it happened that he was in the city on the occasion of the annual banquet, and so, as any other officer of the guard, he had been invited to join the feast.

He remembered The Queen from their days playing together as children, although that was now long ago. He had seen her rarely in the years since, and even then, only from a distance. Now he watched from the corner of his eye as he ate. It seemed to Guylin, as he watched, that she ate not so much for her own benefit as for the benefit of others. She would eat a modest amount to suffice and then hold her cutlery to one side while she talked and listened to those who sat nearby. Only when all had taken their fill around her would she put down her fork and the servants would take the used dishes away.

The musical entertainment was provided by the chief musician and the Palace Orchestra. The court musician had taught The Queen music as a child and was said to be The Queen's favourite eccentric. His mode of dress was by royal indulgence. His shirt tails had never come to agreement between them on the relative virtues of being worn in or out, and the court barber had long since abandoned the futile practice of sending reminder notes.

He would travel far and wide in search of tunes to arrange or which might inspire him, returning from his travels with his leather satchel over his shoulder brim full and overflowing with his scrawled notes. He would always tell his audience the sources of his inspiration, whether it be the love song of an upland shepherdess which he had heard played on a clay whistle, or his own delight at the sight of the first daisies of springtime.

Whilst his facial expressions could be surprising in conversation, in the course of performance they would assume new and dramatic proportions. He could appear positively terrified at the prospect that first violin might miss her cue (for which concern she had never given him cause), and be delighted when the oboe did not.

He would conduct his audience as well as his orchestra, letting them know when they might or might not applaud and to what degree. In those pieces with a particularly stirring finale, his face would assume all the ecstasy of a warrior in the full throes of battle fury as he would rouse his players to put heart and soul into the final bars of his cherished masterpiece.

Whilst his musical talent was undoubted and appreciated, there was still room for debate as to whether his performances provided greater entertainment for the deaf or the blind.

When the music was played for her guests, The Queen would appear as though transformed and transported to another world. The court musician had taught her well. Her tastes were known to be refined and the players were skilled. It was at The Queen's insistence that the music was played only between the courses and not while her guests ate. She would fall still and listen to every note until the piece was finished, and only then she would return her attention to the world of those in her company.

It was said by the common folk of the country that their queen was as fair as a butterfly. To Guylin's eyes, she appeared as frail as one, too, as if one could reach out and crush her with a hand.

Chapter 11

That evening Guylin climbed the stairs that led to a room high in a tower of the palace where Darmid made his study. Guylin knocked on the door, and a few seconds later, the old man answered, looking a little surprised at the arrival of such an unexpected guest. He offered Guylin a seat and Guylin accepted the invitation. Darmid sat behind his desk and asked, "How can I help you?"

Guylin came straight to the point and said, "I have come to enquire what you might tell me about a thunder rose."

The old man laughed at the directness of the question but looked back and said, "And why do you wish to know about that?"

Guylin took no offence at the question and replied politely enough, "The Queen has said that she wishes to have one and that without one, she will not marry. I do not wish to see her alone."

Darmid looked at Guylin. There was something lurking behind Guylin's eyes that Darmid had never been able to fathom and that he could not fathom now. At length, Darmid said, "It is a myth, a fantasy, a dream. Do you not think that you are a little old for dreams?"

Guylin smiled. "I know very well that The Queen would never marry me," he said, "and I would not ask her to. But I remember her as a child. She was kind then, and I have no reason to believe that she is other than that now. Besides, I believe that I may owe my life to her. This would be the least I could do."

Another silence followed while the old man studied Guylin's face, but Guylin's face showed nothing. At last,

Darmid picked up the book that he had been reading when Guylin came in. He said, "If you are asking me to tell you where lightning will strike, then who can know that?" With that, Darmid opened his book and began to read to indicate that he saw no further purpose in the conversation and that as far as he was concerned, the interview was at an end.

Guylin, whether from stubbornness or obtuseness, did not take the hint and sat while the old man read.

At length, Darmid closed his book and said, "Guylin, you did not come here to talk to me about dreams. What have you come to say?"

Guylin smiled again. He said, "My friends in the army once told me of a woman who rides in the mountains. They said lightning comes from the horse's hooves."

"What colour is the horse?" Asked Darmid, frowning.

"Black." Said Guylin, pleased to have piqued the old man's interest.

"And what does the woman wear?" Asked Darmid.

"A great black cloak. It covers her entirely." Said Guylin. "Do you know of her?"

Darmid sighed wearily and put down his book. He said, "She is a different kind of dream. Her realm is in the northern regions. There they call her the Nightmare, and other names besides. A fell creature. An omen of ill."

"Whereabouts in the northern regions?" Asked Guylin.

"Guylin, your friends would send you to pick roses in the garden of the Storm Queen." Said Darmid.

"But if I could find where she would pass," said Guylin, "then perhaps I could find where the lightning would strike!"

"You listen with one ear and not the other," said Darmid impatiently. "Did I not tell you she is an omen of ill? Those who seek her find only madness and death. They say she has a throne made of the bones of poets and fools. Which one are you?"

Guylin started to laugh, much to the old man's irritation. "What are you laughing at?" said Darmid. Guylin stilled his laughter and when he had, he said, "You must call me a fool. My father always said that my poetry was terrible."

***

It was late when Guylin left, and the following afternoon, after his duties were completed for the day, Guylin attended at the office of his commander to request a period of leave.

His commanding officer was Gorald. Guylin and Gorald had joined the guard together in their youth and whilst Guylin had been promoted to office first, he had not been promoted since, while Gorald had risen steadily through the ranks and was now Guylin's commander.

Gorald listened and agreed to Guylin's request for leave. He told him he might return in three days to collect his papers.

So it was in the morning three days later that Guylin returned to Gorald's office at the side of the central courtyard of the palace.

As soon as Guylin had collected his papers and left Gorald's office, the captain of the Royal Guard entered the room. Gorald stood and the captain asked him what Guylin had wanted.

Gorald explained, "He successfully completed an assignment last year. He was promised an extended period of leave." The captain said nothing.

Gorald had a fondness for Guylin, a fondness which he did not extend to the captain. Gorald said coldly, "I am fully aware of the policy regarding his promotion. He is at least entitled to a period of leave."

The captain was looking through the window as Guylin walked towards his horse. "You know what they say of him?" he said.

Gorald refused to be drawn and said irritably, "I try not to listen to any rumours about my men. I do not find them helpful."

The captain continued to watch Guylin. "He is wasting his time," he said, "She will never marry him."

Gorald stood by the captain, looking out of the window at Guylin's back. "She may not have a choice", he said brightly, "if he brings her what she has demanded."

In the courtyard, Guylin tightened the straps of his saddle and adjusted the saddlebags. When he had finished, Guylin looked up to a window above the far side of the courtyard. Within her room, Elzbet stood back from the window as if struck by a dart and let go the curtain from her hand.

She turned slowly away from the window to walk to her dressing room. There, in pride of place, on a carved and polished table in the centre of the room, stood the dolls house. She had brought it with her after all. She looked over its furniture, its chairs, dressers and wardrobes, its carriage and its horses, the exquisite robes, dresses and the dolls themselves. As she did, tears welled up in her eyes until she sobbed, "Daddy, why did you do this to me? I loved you so much." Then burst into her daily flood of tears.

Chapter 12

It was a fine and warm spring day when Guylin set out on his journey. Birds were singing in the blooming trees and the sun was shining. With the mild weather after the heavy winter snows, the waterfalls would be in spate, and Guylin always loved to see waterfalls.

He rode through the city streets, his horse's hooves clipping and clopping on the cobbles as he headed for the hills.

Guylin had never been on a vacation before, and he was looking forward to it. He had brought pencils and paper in case he wanted to try his hand at sketching. He had brought pens in case he had any thoughts that he might wish to record and had a mandolin to play in the evenings.

Guylin rode with his sword at his side. Regulations permitted him to wear civilian clothes on a private journey if he so wished, but Guylin had chosen to wear his uniform instead. He felt it afforded him an added degree of protection. Bandits might think more carefully before approaching an armed soldier. Besides that, his uniform was very smart and he felt rather proud of it.

Before long, the road had taken him from the city and he was riding on the rim of the valley, on roads that led north. He knew the direction in which he was travelling, but apart from that, he had no specific plan. Whenever he came to a crossroads, he would follow whichever road seemed to be the most pleasant. Sometimes he would ask his horse which way it wanted to go. Guylin's preference was generally for the higher paths, but his horse seemed to prefer the level riverside ways. As a compromise, they did a little of both, and so they made their way.

In the evenings, Guylin sat in the inns to take his supper. Afterwards, he would take out his mandolin to play with whomsoever would arrive with an instrument or a voice to sing and might wish to join him. Although, at first, Guylin did not know the local folk songs that the people in the villages liked to play, he was able to improvise and soon learnt their styles and tunes.

In the mornings, he would resume his journey, travelling further and further away from places with which he was familiar and into regions where few amongst his friends had ever ventured.

The roads were narrow and the mountain paths were steep. There were often long stretches of wild and untamed land before Guylin would come to a village with an inn at which he might spend the night.

One evening, he was sitting after his supper with a group who were regulars in the inn. One played a fiddle, one a drum, one played a flute and one was a lively singer who played a bass mandolin. The singer was quite adept at encouraging his listeners to join in and to sing along.

They had already played several of the popular local classics and ballads, and quite a crowd had grown around them. The singer was wondering what to play next. He looked to Guylin and at his uniform and then said, "If you're a queen's soldier, then here's a song for you. A song for yer lady."

He nodded to the others and began to play a song that they quickly joined. The singer looked to Guylin to see if he knew the song, but Guylin did not. However, the chords and structure were straightforward enough, and Guylin was able to play along as the song started and the singer began to sing.

"In the high mountain peaks
Where the sun shines but no flower grows
In the rocks and the ice

Stands the bud of the fair mountain rose.
What sun would thaw
These mountain snows
And see the bloom
Of the Maiden Rose?

Morning is her train
Dawn is the gold of her flowing robes
Softer than the summer rain
The high wind blows and the river flows
And they call
'What sun would thaw
These mountain snows
And see the bloom
Of the Maiden Rose?'"

Guylin had been concentrating on the chords and on keeping rhythm. It was only now when the instrumental break began that he realised the subject of their song. With the flute and fiddle playing a crescendo and the listeners clapping in time, Guylin laid aside his mandolin and sat, feeling suddenly out of place in his formal uniform amongst the stamping, singing villagers in their simple working clothes.

The singer took up the song once again for the final verse, with all singing along.

"What heart would brave the steep mountainside
And win the rose as his own smiling bride?
And still they ask
'What sun would thaw
These cold and lonely mountain snows
And when will bloom (two, three, four, one, two, three…)
This Maiden Rose?'"

The singer finished the song with a spirited flourish of chords amidst applause and then turned to see how their visitor had enjoyed their tune. But by then, their guest had gone.

***

Storms raged in the night and rain lashed the windows. Crows screeched evil omens upon the wind. On his bed, Guylin snored softly as he slept.

Chapter 13

By morning, the clouds had cleared from the sky and clear sunlight shone on the puddles of rain. Guylin saddled his horse and resumed his journey.

At each new stop on the way, he would ask the people whom he met if any knew of the woman who rode cloaked upon a black horse. Some laughed and told him stories to frighten children. Others went pale and cold, and said they did not speak of such things in those parts, until Guylin stopped asking and simply continued his journey northwards.

He was now travelling in remote parts of the country where The Queen's rule was acknowledged only grudgingly at best. The views of the mountain peaks that he saw from the ridges thrilled the heart, and the flowers of the valley floor were a delight to the senses.

One evening, Guylin sat at a table in an inn. He had just finished a bowl of soup and was writing some notes on the paper that he had brought with him when a man came and stood before him. The man tucked his thumbs into his belt and looked up and down Guylin's uniform. He did not introduce himself but asked in a menacing tone,

"What's with the shiny buttons?"

Guylin looked up and smiled pleasantly, despite the man's manner. He replied, "It is my uniform. I am an officer in the Royal Guard."

The man sneered and huffed derisively, "One of Her Majesty's boys." Guylin did not respond, and the man said, "Is it true she poisoned her own father and brothers?"

Guylin glanced to either side to see if anyone else in the inn was paying attention to the exchange, but he could not tell. The man was seeking to provoke and Guylin did not desire a fight. He looked back to the man who stood before him. He was thickset and wore a long knife in his belt, which was common enough in those parts for any workman or for any whose day might take him to walk alone in the hills. Guylin wore his sword at his side but wished to avoid unsheathing it in the tight confines of the low-ceilinged inn.

"No," said Guylin quietly. "That is not true."

"Well, that's what they say 'round here," the man said, standing his ground.

Guylin looked around one more time, but still he could not be sure if anyone listening would come to the man's side if there were a conflict. Guylin reached out his hand to the neck of his mandolin.

"Is that your drum?" Guylin asked, nodding towards a flat goatskin drum that sat on a bench by the wall.

The man was a little taken by surprise. "Yes," he said uncertainly.

Guylin said, "If you can match me song for song and drink for drink, then I will pay for your drinking tonight. But if you cannot, then by the end of the night, you will join me in drinking to Her Majesty The Queen's good health."

Before the stranger could reply, the landlord had placed a bottle on the table that stood between the two men and said, "That is the most sensible thing I have heard all day." He turned his eyes to the large man and said, "We don't want any trouble here tonight, Jed."

A short while and several songs later, Guylin was sitting in the company of an impromptu band that had gathered to play and sing. Jed, with his drum, did not seem to have noticed that Guylin was not drinking as much as Jed was drinking, or if he had noticed, he did not seem to care too much as Guylin was paying for more than his share.

There was a break between the songs and the laughter, and Jed wanted to talk about politics, a subject that Guylin had been trying to avoid.

"If I was queen," said Jed slurring only slightly, "I wouldn't do the things that she does."

"Would you not," said Guylin strumming a chord, hoping that someone might share his distaste for political debate and would join him to begin another tune.

"Nah," said Jed, then he said indignantly, "Do you know she taxes farmers on seed corn?"

"I did not know that," said Guylin sympathetically.

"Yes. And what does she spend it on?" Jed asked the group rhetorically. "Schools for kids! You don't grow wheat by reading to it!"

After some more singing and a few more drinks, the landlord announced that the evening was finished and it was time for everyone to go to their homes. Guylin's companions were just about to drain their cups to leave when Guylin said to Jed, "Are you not forgetting something?"

Jed and the others looked up quizzically. "Forgetting what?" said Jed.

"To drink to the health of Her Majesty The Queen," said Guylin calmly.

Jed laughed and said, "Why should I?" looking around at his friends in the inn.

Guylin waited for the laughter to finish before explaining patiently, "Because I am an armed officer in the service of The Queen and it is my duty to defend the honour of The Queen by whatever means I deem fit."

The room had fallen suddenly quiet. Jed looked at Guylin and Guylin returned his gaze, steady and unflinching. Jed looked from the corner of his eyes to the others in the room. There might have been twenty of them, but Guylin looked only at Jed. Jed's companions were waiting uneasily to see how Jed would react.

Jed sat for a moment without responding, then reached out and took his cup in hand. He raised it and said formally, "To the very good health of Her Majesty The Queen."

Guylin raised his cup and replied politely, "And to your very good health, too."

***

Although Guylin had left the saddle on his horse and had planned to go for a ride around the lake by the village after his supper, it was now far too late for that. It was dark, it was raining and whilst he had not drunk as much as his companions, he had drunk more than he had planned to drink and rather more than he was accustomed.

The landlord took a lamp and offered to accompany Guylin outside to see to his horse.

Outside, Guylin did not take shelter under the eaves of the inn as they walked through the yard to the stables. The cool breeze and the cold drops of rain were pleasant and refreshing after the snug warmth of the inn and Guylin felt they might clear his head. He picked his way over the wet flags where the rivulets trickled between while the innkeeper's lamp bobbed ahead. Guylin waited at the stable door and looked at the silhouettes of the hills and peaks while the innkeeper searched his large iron ring for the key. There was a distant rumble in the sky.

"What is that?" asked Guylin. It did not seem to be raining hard enough for a thunderstorm and he wondered if perhaps it was the sound of icefall in the mountains with the spring thaw.

The innkeeper did not look up from his keyring. "She's riding," he snorted.

"Who?" said Guylin.

"The witch," said the innkeeper with distaste as he found his key and unlocked the stable door. He seemed keen to get back inside. "The night hag."

Guylin took a second to understand what the man had said, then ran through the stable door, directly to his horse. He unhitched the reins and, still running, led the horse from the stall. Once outside, he jumped into the saddle and, ignoring the innkeeper's calls, he rode full tilt through the slumbering village.

There was little light from the moon that showed through cracks in the clouds behind him and Guylin could only hope that the horse could see where it was going. Water and mud splashed up from the village street. At the end of the village, Guylin halted the horse to peer into the darkness to see the way. One path led to the lake and the road beyond. Another led to the high mountain pastures. Guylin set the horse running to the path to the mountain. Lightning flashed, giving a moment of illumination. A few seconds later, thunder rolled.

Rain was falling more heavily now on Guylin's head and neck as he and the horse climbed. They leapt over a shallow stream that ran over the stones of the path and the horse began to gallop on a narrow sheep trail into the hills.

Clouds shifted before the moon and Guylin could scarcely see where he was going. He shook his head to clear the haze within as another burst of lightning lit the sky.

In the flash, he saw that he was at the foot of a steep bank of scree, the top of which was lost against the sky. The bank was too steep and the rock too loose for the horse to climb. Guylin leapt from the saddle to begin to scramble upwards on the rolling, tumbling stones, leaving the horse on the hillside far below. The rain soaked through his clothes and the sharp rock cut his hands. His feet slipped and slipped again, but they pushed him still higher and higher and his lungs gasped to catch breath as he climbed.

By the time Guylin had hauled himself to the top of the scar, the rain had almost stopped. His clothes were sodden and his hands were raw. His heart was beating fast. He stood in a stupor of exhaustion, staring before him, but there was nothing to see on the ridge apart from the black void of the valley and an overhanging cliff above.

He was dizzy. His chest heaved and his legs were shaking from the effort. His eyes were damp and stinging and his throat was tight from his folly and frustration.

He stood there panting and unsure what to do. He had abandoned his horse at the foot of the cliff and all that he owned was on it. To climb down the wet slope in the darkness would be more dangerous than even the ascent and the attempt would only be madness. Even if he did, who was to say if he would ever find his horse in the darkness? He was cold, wet with rain and sweat, and he started to shiver.

From behind him, the faint moonlight glinted through the breaking clouds upon the mouth of a dingy cave beneath the crag. Perhaps there he might at least find some shelter to sit out the night until enough light came for him to find his way back to the village.

A new bout of rain began to fall, but Guylin was unaware and it made little difference to his drenched shirt. The wind wailed "Ah woe!" and the rain mocked his tears, but Guylin heard nothing, felt nothing and saw nothing as his eyes strained to pierce the thick gloom of the cave. He could not even see the ground beneath his feet as he entered.

Suddenly, the air turned blue with light and the cave roared as a deafening crack shocked the ground. The mountain shuddered and Guylin spun about. There he saw it in the mouth of the cave, a pure white rose shining with its own light, a curving plume of vapour rising around it. For a moment, Guylin stood frozen as he stared at the prize he sought, while the thunder crashed and rolled about him. Then he pulled himself forward, knelt down and plucked the rose from the ground, roots and all, still steaming in his hands while the thunder echoed through the valley below, until the last echo of thunder was gone. The water dripping at the mouth of the cave babbled in the whistle of the wind and Guylin stared at the perfect treasure he held in his hands.

It was beautiful beyond imagining and from it came a scent to arouse the soul.

Something made Guylin shiver and feel sick to the stomach; it was not from the drinking, nor was it from his exertions before. Guylin looked up from where he crouched and saw before him, in the moonlight, a horse that waited on the ridge from where Guylin had climbed. Guylin stood up.

There was no rider upon the horse and the horse was not his own. Now Guylin saw standing near him, by the mouth of the cave, a figure of a woman covered entirely in a great black cloak. A hood covered her face. Guylin stared, unable to move. The woman raised up her pale white hands to lift the hood from before her. Her face was as cold as the moon and her eyes were as vast and empty as the night. Guylin opened his mouth wide to scream, but his voice was stolen by the wind and rain.

Chapter 14

When Guylin did not report for duty on the day set for his return, he was at first declared absent without leave.

Some villagers had found his horse wandering and taken it to the inn where Guylin had been drinking that night. The innkeeper tended it there until a passing troop came through the region and the innkeeper passed it over to their safekeeping.

When the news of the horse was brought back to the city, Guylin was declared missing and not absent. The court gossips wove witty stories and embellished jokes with tales about the officer of the guard who had gone riding while drunk and had fallen off his horse into a ravine.

The Queen was informed as she was informed of all important news. She made no comment, but, nonetheless, none felt it appropriate to share with her the stories, jokes and gossip.

Spring ended and summer brought the excitement of the fair. New stories drove out the old and the tongues of the court found new titbits to set them wagging. Guylin's name passed from their lips even as summer ended. The workers brought in the produce from the orchards and hillside fields and still nothing was heard or seen of Guylin.

One day, The Queen was sitting in her court. She had heard all of the business that was scheduled for the morning—the civil projects, questions of justice, foreign news and any matters that required her decision or comment—and she asked if there was any new business for her to hear. The Court Chamberlain said that there was indeed one new matter.

"Your Majesty may recall that one of the officers of the Royal Guard has been missing for some time. No doubt Your Majesty will be pleased to hear that he has returned safely to the palace early this morning. However, as his absence has been without leave and as he is an officer of the Royal Guard, the case of his absence falls to Your Majesty to hear, if Your Majesty will hear it."

For a moment, The Queen seemed to be taken by surprise and unsure how to answer.

The ears of the ladies of court pricked up at the chamberlain's announcement. It had not been so long ago that tales of Guylin had been hot on everyone's lips. To be in court on the day that the story came back to life was a treat, the tale of which would make all of their friends jealous. Besides that, The Queen's reaction was a tale in itself. It was rare, if ever, that The Queen showed any sign of emotion, and there was a strong rumour that The Queen had something of a soft spot for this particular officer.

The Queen said yes, she would hear the case. The ladies looked to each other and to The Queen who had recovered from her momentary lack of composure, and they watched her as Guylin was summoned and brought to the room.

He was led in flanked by two armed guards and brought to the middle of the court before the throne on its raised platform. His hair had been cut that morning and his beard had been trimmed. He had washed and had been provided with a fresh uniform for him to be presented to The Queen, although he himself appeared weathered from his time away and on the road. As a man on trial, he did not carry a sword.

The ladies were looking to The Queen to see what would be her reaction to his reappearance. Although she said nothing, her visible smile of relief at seeing Guylin was, if anything, quite endearing. Guylin, for his part, stood with his eyes cast appropriately downwards.

The Queen stifled her smile and asked soberly, "Has he offered any explanation for his absence?"

"Your Majesty, he has not," said the chamberlain. "In fact, he has not said a word to anyone. But it does appear that he has a gift that he wishes to give to Your Majesty."

"A gift?" said The Queen in surprise, then bit her lip. It was not her practice simply to repeat the words of others.

"Indeed," said the chamberlain. "If Your Majesty would care to receive it."

"Well, yes," said The Queen with a pleasant smile. "We are always pleased to receive gifts."

The men who were present feigned indifference, but the ladies found the events most entertaining and looked on eagerly to see what would be the gift of the silent and errant soldier. The chamberlain instructed an attendant to take Guylin's gift from his hand and to deliver it to The Queen.

The attendant approached Guylin who reached down to the place on his belt where ordinarily his sword would hang. From there, he untied a long white leather bag, which he gave to the servant to give to The Queen. The servant took the bag and approached the steps that led to the throne. Guylin returned his eyes to the floor.

Even the men were finding it hard to disguise their interest as the attendant climbed the steps to the throne to deliver Guylin's gift. The Queen hesitated only slightly before accepting the bag from the servant's hand. She took it and laid it in her lap as the ladies craned their necks to see her untie the strings.

As she did, a faint fragrance emerged from within. A subtle, beautiful and unworldly scent filled the room whilst all looked to see what was inside the bag. One of the ladies giggled as the white and perfect rose was revealed. Another gasped as she realised what The Queen held in her now trembling hands.

The rose was as beautiful as The Queen herself. Pure and unblemished, it shone with a light that reflected in The Queen's face and lit her eyes with a delight that passed all earthly cares. It was as whole and as fresh as if it yet grew. There were still drops of rain upon its petals and leaves.

Elzbet gazed upon it, then lifted her eyes and looked around the room at those who stood before her. The ladies stared open-eyed and open-mouthed at her shining face. Of the men, some looked confused, while others glared in undisguised rage.

Only Guylin did not look to The Queen but stood with his eyes still cast to the floor until The Queen's gaze lit upon him. Only then did he look up, and even when he did, his eyes made no demand of her. He had offered his queen a gift and nothing more.

Elzbet looked at him. While she did, she appeared as one who had found calm and refuge amidst the very heart of the storm yet feared the storm still. A silent minute passed with the eyes of all upon her until she looked down to the rose that she held and at its simple and awesome beauty. Carefully and meticulously, slowly, as if she did not trust her hands, she placed the rose back into its bag. She did not tie its cords but handed the bag to the attendant by her side.

"It is very beautiful," she said quietly, almost to herself, her voice quavering. She could feel eyes burning upon her. She looked up at the members of her court who were waiting to hear her words. "We shall certainly look after it," she said a little louder, but her voice still shook.

The court chamberlain, ever a man of delicate discretion, broke the long silence that ensued and said, "Will Your Majesty now hear his case?"

For a moment, The Queen did not appear to understand the question and did not react or respond, then she said stiffly, "He has given me a gift. I cannot judge his case."

Again, there was silence until the chamberlain spoke. He said, "Then perhaps his commanding officer should hear the case?"

"Yes," said The Queen. "His commanding officer should hear the case."

With that, she stood to leave the court. She appeared flushed and eager to be away. Those in attendance had barely time to bow or curtsy before The Queen walked from the throne to the door. The doormen opened the doors and the retinue hurried to fall into line behind.

Once outside and with the doors closed behind them, one of the ladies-in-waiting could contain herself no longer. She cried excitedly, "He has given Your Majesty a thunder rose!" Elzbet turned and snapped in sudden anger, "I did not ask him to. I did not ask anyone to!" The fury that flashed from her face silenced any response and Elzbet walked in a blazing storm to her private apartments while her retinue walked a pace more than usual behind.

At the entrance to her rooms, her fury had barely abated. With forced calm, she told her attendants, "I need to be alone for an hour or so. I will call for you," before she turned and entered her room.

The guards on duty closed the doors behind her. Those in her retinue looked to each other, uncertain as to what they were to do. It was at least clear that they had been dismissed for the hour and so each went quietly his or her way to await The Queen's summons to return, leaving only the two guards on duty outside the door.

For a long time, there were few sounds heard from within, then for as long, only silence until, at last, the door opened by barely a crack. One of the doormen approached the door to see what The Queen might require. The Queen's face was hidden, but the guard heard her voice, quiet and unsteady. "Would you please bring me my rose," she said.. "The one that the officer gave to me." Then she closed the door.

Neither of the guards knew to what The Queen referred and so one remained on duty while the other left to seek one who might know. He returned after a few minutes and knocked gently on the door. A second later, the door opened but again only slightly. The doorman held out the white leather bag. From within, Elzbet reached out her hand to take the bag from him. "Thank you very much," she said so softly as barely to be heard, then as softly closed the door.

Now you ask, "Did The Queen cry when she entered the room?" She did not cry, she howled, with a bolster pressed to her face to stifle her pained screams until all her tears were spent. Then weary, she took a sheet from her bed and placed it on the mirror that stood by the table. For why should she look once more on red eyes?

"During the silence, what did she do then?" She sat on her bed with her tears and thoughts, stared long at the hand she held in her lap, the hand that had so briefly held the rose, then pressed it hard to her mouth and breathed in, sobbing and gasping to breathe the pure scent. She turned her hand, now this way and now that, to find where the scent lingered most strongly, to catch each faint trace, the beautiful scent of the fair rose her hand had touched and held. Again, again, yet again she breathed deep till her heart had calmed enough now to ask at the door, "Would you please bring me my rose."

She moved a chair beside the door, waited, still smelling her hand, till, at last, it came. And when it came, she took the rose, placed it in her most precious vase on the table. Then she took the sheet from off the mirror. She returned it neatly onto her bed.

"And when the bed was made, what did she do?" She stood there to see herself reflected in her mirror, with her rose before her, or held to her side, or clutched to her breast. All else she did that day was with her rose.

"And did she sleep that night?" Never better. She woke once and looked up to see her rose with moonlight shining on its pure clear drops, then turned to sleep, contented till the day.

"And were there tears that day?" Only of joy and pride, for who had a rose such as she? Who had a lover so true as Guylin?

Chapter 15

The following day, Gorald sat in his office, looking at the papers on the desk, cursing his fortunes and wondering why he of all people was charged with this task.

Guylin sat before him, quiet and reflective as though nothing were amiss, whilst Gorald read the papers. There was little to read. Guylin's record was unblemished before his absence and Gorald knew the facts of the story perfectly well.

Gorald put the papers down and looked at Guylin. He had still not said a word to anyone since his return. Gorald had no instructions directly from The Queen. She had not called for her staff after an hour yesterday, nor indeed throughout the rest of the day. She had come down late that morning and when she did, she made no mention to anyone of the events of the previous day.

At last, Gorald asked, "Can you talk?"

Guylin looked up. "Yes," he replied, pleasantly and politely.

Gorald said, "You have been away for six months. Can you tell me where you have been all this time?"

Guylin pondered the question for a few moments and then said, "No."

Gorald sucked in his breath and ground his teeth. He tried to scrutinise Guylin's face. He had known Guylin since their youth. There was no insolence in his voice nor was there any in his demeanour. He had been asked a straightforward question and he had given a truthful answer.

Gorald looked down to his papers and drummed his fingers on the desk as he considered and silently cursed again. His instructions were simply to remove Guylin as far from the palace as possible, as quickly as possible. If anyone wanted to interrogate Guylin for answers, it was their affair and they could do it themselves. It was not in Gorald's brief and Gorald was not going to press for answers if none were forthcoming.

Eventually, he said, "I am not going to strip you of your rank, but I can hardly expect men to follow your commands."

Guylin did not offer any comment and so Gorald continued, "We always need men on patrol in the hills. You will serve there until The Queen or I reconsider your case."

With that, the matter was concluded and Guylin was dismissed. He was to be sent to join a company of men in a distant area that was a feared haunt of bandits and raiders who would take refuge in its labyrinthine passes. Guylin accepted the posting without protest and left later that day to join his new company.

The others of the troop that Guylin joined were a mix of rough young men from around the country. Each one had a tale of his own to tell of how he had come to be assigned to so remote a post.

Guylin talked little with them and kept himself to himself, and his new companions allowed him his privacy. They respected Guylin's silence and welcomed his presence and experience. With time, Guylin gave them confidence, and with Guylin in their company, they would take on tasks at which others would balk, sometimes riding out altogether and returning a day or so later with some notorious and wanted outlaw strapped to a saddle. Guylin was a man of ability upon whom they could rely in the never-ending fight against banditry.

There were other times when his presence was not required, that Guylin would ride out by himself and only return a few days later when he was next required to resume his duties. And so the winter months passed.

Chapter 16

The winter was bitter cold, but spring came at last, bringing the thaw to the valleys whilst snow still lay on the mountain peaks.

A trapper and his young apprentice had been camping in the forests near the eastern border. The apprentice was called Jacko, and he was taking an early morning stroll to loosen his stiff back and legs after a night of broken sleep on the cold forest floor. His master's name was Victor. Victor was seasoned to life out of doors, and Jacko had left Victor snoring and sleeping soundly in the tent.

Jacko had lost his way in the forest somewhat, but he was not concerned. They had made their camp by a stream, and as long as Jacko could find the stream, he was sure to find the tent and Victor.

Jacko's walk took him out through a clump of trees and into the sunshine on a rocky outcrop that looked down on to the country's eastern gate. However, instead of the tranquil morning traffic he might have expected, with travellers on foot and the border soldiers checking the cargo of some foreign merchant's train, what Jacko saw appalled him. The gates lay smashed and hanging loose from shattered stone pillars. A huge ram shod with iron swung on chains suspended from a covered frame on rollers. Men lay slain upon the ramparts above and a vast army of men on horseback stood outside. Whatever battle there had been that morning had been swift and bloody and had only just finished. Riders were even now returning to the ruins of the gateway from the road where men lay slaughtered, cut down as they had run or with arrows in their backs.

Jacko turned and ran back into the woods to escape from sight. He must warn Victor and raise the alarm. He found the stream and raced along its bank, running headlong into a clearing where he skidded to a halt. Before him in the clearing sat a man in armour on a heavy horse. The man turned around at the sound of Jacko's approach and turned his steed to face him. Jacko looked around, but there was nowhere to run. The rider took out a long-handled mace and Jacko took his long knife from his belt, then the rider spurred his horse towards his prey. The horse's hooves shook the ground as the horse approached. Jacko danced on his toes, holding the knife aloft, waiting for the deadly onslaught. Suddenly, the horse tumbled forward, Victor's arrow through its flank. The rider flew through the air, flailing wildly as he crashed to the ground by the stump of a tree. Before he could rise, Jacko ran forward and worked the tip of his knife in between the struggling rider's helmet and breastplate until the blood spurted out, the breath rattled in his chest and the rider fell still.

When Jacko looked up, he saw Victor approaching with his hunting bow and quiver. As loudly as he dared, Jacko said, "The country has been invaded! We must raise the alarm!"

The two men ran, with Victor leading the short way to the camp to collect flint and tinder. Jacko was freezing cold and shaking as they ran up the steep paths to find the beacon. They saw no one on the ascent and at the summit, they found the stored kindling and fuel. Victor built up the pyre while Jacko tried to light the kindling. His hands shook so badly that he could barely hold the knife and flint, and so Victor took them from him. Before long, he had a live flame in the nest of dry tinder. He put the tinder to the straw, and when the flames had turned to a blaze, he climbed the ladder and put the straw to the pyre.

The two kept watch near the beacon until the flicker of an answering flame was showing two miles to the west and another could be seen in the south.

It was close to noon when a guard on the city wall saw a pillar of smoke rising beyond the hills to the east. He called a sergeant, who sent out messengers on horseback to report. They rode back shortly afterwards, blowing trumpets to raise the alarm. Beacons were blazing all across the east. The border had been breached.

Bells rang in the city and trumpets were blown in the valleys. Soldiers hurried to report for duty and all leave was cancelled. Shopkeepers put away their wares, closed up shop and ran home to fetch armour and weapons. From the fields, men came in to put down hoes and to take up pikes and spears.

Word came in the afternoon with the swift riders of the postal service on panting horses, reporting the enemy's number and order. The invaders were wild men from the north who must have travelled more than a month to come through the empty wastelands to reach the borders of the little kingdom. The enemy numbered forty thousand or more on horseback. They came with catapults, ladders, engines and the ram that had broken the eastern gate. The enemy was led by their warlord. He was ill famed, cruel and arrogant. He had boasted that no city could stand before him. Great cities with high walls had been broken by his hordes. They had devastated kingdoms and laid whole cities to waste for plunder.

Faces in the city turned ashen grey, sick with fear at the mention of his name. The city's walls were built to protect against thieves from the hills or an attack by an army of a rival mountain clan, not an invasion from abroad. The people of the land had always looked to the mountains to protect them. But now the enemy already held a long stretch of the main trade road and the lanes on either side were in their grasp. The road had brought prosperity to the little kingdom, but now the little kingdom's wealth had caught the enemy's greedy eye and its wide trade road was bringing the enemy to its very heart.

At night, those who sought flight prepared to depart: merchants whose servants spent the dark hours packing and ambassadors who had sent letters of excuse to the palace that day. The letters assured The Queen of their imminent return and that they had already dispatched requests to their monarch's for support. The Queen, busy with her council of war, granted them leave without audience, thanking each for their pledge of support. But for all the good wishes and pledges, it was known that the nearest allied troop would take three weeks to arrive if they came at all, and the enemy would be at the gates in two days if unchecked.

With the first light of day, they took to the roads heading west, and after the merchants and ambassadors, those with relatives or friends in remote parts sent away their wives and children with the promise to send for them when peace returned. But however many left, more came, preferring such protection as the city's walls could afford them to the exposed mountain farmsteads and open villages. On every road and through every gate they came. Men pushed carts with the jumbled goods of their household, clothes and blankets, pots and pans, coins and jewels stuffed in their pockets, while their wives ran with babies in arms, a string of children holding hands behind.

Before long, thousands filled every road leading towards the city, scurrying frantically to bring themselves within its walls. Some were silent and frightened, others were panicking and hysterical. Soldiers in the street moved all along to clear the way for others who arrived. They ordered men to leave their wives and carts, to run to the armoury for helmets, bucklers, swords and spears and to report for duty. From there, they were dispatched, some to the walls and some to defensive positions in the hills and passes. Those who were sent to the hills were ordered to keep off the road, to use the farmers' tracks and secret ways, to leave the main road clear for those who came to the city. They would be given instructions when they reached their posts. Others were sent with quartermasters to ride out with wagons and axes, to break open stores to bring in grain to lay up for the siege.

Two large inns near the city gates were designated as hospitals and those with skills to tend the sick were called there to await the wounded. Pavilions were set up on every green space and on the lawn of the palace with blankets for those who might need.

In the afternoon, the first wave of refugees arrived. Footsore and weary, they had walked through the night, not daring to sleep on the way exposed on the bare mountain side. Their children were wide eyed and bewildered. Every door in the town opened to welcome them, with two or three families to every room. Mothers sat nursing on the floor while children huddled in every corner.

It was the mid-afternoon and wagons appeared carrying men lying on beds of straw, those who had been wounded in the skirmishes and attacks on the border, or who had been injured while trying to break up the roads to foul the way for the invading enemy. The wagon drivers stood as they drove, shouting to clear the road to let pass the injured men to bring them to the hospital rooms, and still through every gate, more people came in terrified flight.

Darmid weaved through the pressing, pushing crowd and the panic of the streets until he had found his way to the hospital. When he arrived, he came to the wounded men one by one, offering what help he could, giving directions and orders for the care of the injured and dying, and hearing the accounts of those who had brought in their comrades and friends.

He had been there several hours and had seen almost all of the men when he came, at last, to where Guylin lay. Guylin's gashes had been cleaned and sewn, but he was pale and unconscious and had lost much blood. The two men of his troop who had brought him told how they had rescued him from the enemy's hands. Darmid listened to their account and looked over Guylin's wounds. He gave orders for his care, that he be closely tended in a room by himself and that the room be kept well aired and warm.

By the time Darmid left the hospital, it was close to evening. The streets were almost empty. Only the last weary stragglers still stumbled through the closing gates. No children played outside. The men waited on the walls or in the hills, and the enemy had made camp in a trough of land between two mountain ridges a day's march to the east of the city.

Darmid hurried to the palace. There he enquired where he might find The Queen. He was told that the council had dispersed and The Queen was taking a rest in a side room. He made his way there directly and spoke to the maid waiting in attendance outside. The maid knocked and entered the room, then returned a minute later to say that Darmid might enter.

Elzbet sat in a gilded chair by the window, looking out over the palace grounds to the streets and hills beyond. The hillside glowed in the last hazy light of day, at peace as it waited for the siege and breaking tide of war.

The Queen did not turn nor acknowledge his presence, and so Darmid waited by the door for The Queen to speak. At length, Elzbet said quietly, "Yes?"

Darmid said as gently as he could, "I have come to tell Your Majesty that Guylin has been injured. He has been treated, but his wounds are very grave."

Darmid waited for The Queen to respond, but all that Elzbet said in reply was "I know". She sat immobile as though her face were made of marble.

The Queen added nothing and so Darmid asked, "Do you believe that he loves you?"

The Queen did not respond to his boldness at first, but then said almost indifferently, "He gave me a rose."

Darmid had no time for pity or patience and he said, "There is no guile in him. No deceit. He tried to lie once when he was a child. His face turned pink and he stammered so badly, he could not finish his sentence. I do not believe he has tried since." Still there was no response and so Darmid said with growing impatience, "He has given Your Majesty all that he has and all that he is. What more would Your Majesty ask of him?"

Elzbet flinched momentarily but sat still as though Darmid had not spoken before she replied in a broken voice, "Forgiveness."

Darmid had not been invited to sit, but he sat, nonetheless, in a chair by the door. He sighed and said rather more sympathetically, "It may not be his to give."

His words pierced and sapped strength from The Queen. Darmid continued, "And besides, what would Your Majesty give in return?"

Elzbet now looked away from the window and with no attempt to hide the tears on her cheeks, she said to his face with mirthless, bitter anger and irony, "What can I give him? I have nothing!"

Darmid was not cowed under her sharp gaze but maintained his firmness when he said, "Then give to him what he has given you."

The Queen looked at him directly. Darmid sat without speaking for long moments until The Queen wiped the tears from her face and dabbed her eyes with a kerchief. She stood and straightened her dress, then without a word, she left.

Darmid did not follow her. This was not the petulant exit of a wilful child. Darmid stood and, as he so often had before, uttered a prayer for them both before leaving the room to return to his studies.

Chapter 17

Night had fallen and Elzbet sat in a carriage with Elysia, her maid. Elzbet had washed her face, brushed and arranged her hair and had changed her dress. She sat wrapped in a fur-lined cloak and trimmed gloves against the cold of night. Her face showed no sign of her earlier tears.

She sat in silence and Elysia did not speak to disturb her mistress's private thoughts as the carriage rolled through the streets glistening with the dew of night until it had brought Elzbet to the entrance of the hospital.

The carriage stopped and the footman set down stairs outside the carriage door for The Queen to descend. The maid left the carriage first to offer her hand to support her mistress as she stepped down and then escorted The Queen to the door of the building.

It was well lit inside and Elzbet, accompanied by her maid, walked up the stairs and through the corridors until they came to a hallway. There, a doctor was sitting, talking to a nurse. They both rose as The Queen approached. The doctor bowed and the nurse curtsied.

"Is he here?" Elzbet asked the doctor.

The doctor did not ask to whom The Queen referred but replied, "He is, Your Majesty."

"And may I enter?" she asked formally.

"Of course, Your Majesty," the doctor said. He stepped forward to a door to one of the rooms and opened it.

Inside, the room was simple, clean and uncluttered. There was the bed in which Guylin lay beneath sheets and blankets. There was a table and a wooden chair beside. A fire in the hearth kept the room warm and lamps lit every corner.

Once The Queen was inside, the doctor left and closed the door.

Elzbet looked around the room for something she might do to ease Guylin's sleep, but she found nothing. Her heart almost failed when she saw his shallow breathing, but she strengthened herself and drew herself up to say what she had come to say and to do what she had come to do.

Now our storyteller speaks to his listeners and asks, "My dear friends, I pray you promise me this: that you judge not The Queen Elzbet harshly for her actions here. Do not say 'I would...' or 'she should have done somehow otherwise'.

"And sincerely and humbly do I ask, do not judge the paucity of my art. Do not hold me up against past giants whose words could paint a kingdom in the air or mount a nation's battles on a stage, for I am but the impoverished child of a lost and orphaned age. Judge me not, for you will find me wanting in my skill.

"I shall let The Queen Elzbet speak freely. I will tell only her words and her deeds. The passions of her heart I leave to yours.

"And so, judge not my Elzbet's broken words, for these words have dwelt too long in her heart, and her soft heart is breaking.

"Let her speak. Elzbet says..."

"I said a thunder rose would win my heart. I did not believe there was such a thing or that anyone would give one to me. Did you believe, Guylin? Did you have faith? Or were you just faithful? You simply knew that was what your queen said that she wanted.

"You gave me a rose, sweet, beautiful fool.

"I was so angry with you when you did. That you could do such a thing, so foolish.

"Did you think I would ever marry you? Bring you there to that pit of rogues and lies? They would have destroyed you in an instant. They would tear flesh from your bones with their teeth. You never knew how to care for yourself. Even as a child. My friend teased you once. I scolded her so badly for your sake, I would not talk to her for a whole day.

"I thought, 'Which of my friends should he marry?' Someone good, someone clever, someone kind. Pretty. I wanted her to be pretty. I never even thought of you for me.

"I could not think of anyone for you, not that I could trust to love you enough.

"I knew I could trust you with anything. But I could not trust you not to love me.

"Do I love you? Did you give me a choice? Guylin, you are as beautiful as truth, but your love was cruel to my poor heart. I had laid it to rest so long ago. I thought it slept cold and safe in its cage, till the day you wakened it with a rose and shattered its cage of ice forever. I did not even thank you for your gift. I wanted to. I wanted to thank you.

"I put it away safely out of sight, in my treasury, where I would not see.

"But I did see. Every night I saw it, burning and shining in the cold and dark. And each morning, I would wake before dawn and look for it on the bed beside me. My heart would jump and I would leap from bed, put on shoes and run to see it was safe, that it was whole. That it had not faded.

"And it never had. It was always fresh as at the moment you gave it to me. And there I would sit, gazing in wonder and dare myself to dream. And I would know I could lose all that ever I had owned, yet call me rich if I but had my rose.

"Since the day that you gave that rose to me, it has grown around my heart, each day more. With each beat, its thorns have pricked my heartflesh. Yet still my heart beats. Still I breathe. And by my heart's pain alone do I know I live. And would any offer to me some drug or potion to take this pain from my heart, I would only hate him. I love my rose.

"Oh, my sweet Guylin, I wish you would speak!"

He lay there sleeping and did not stir. And so she took from within her cloak the white leather bag and laid it on the table by his bed. Carefully, she untied the strings of the bag.

As she did, the scent of the rose filled the room, subtle and faint, yet infinitely beautiful. She took the rose from the bag. She looked at it in all its pristine perfection, the raindrops glinting on its petals and leaves like precious and intricate jewels shining with the light of the rose.

She laid the rose upon the bag and now began to remove her gloves, finger by finger, baring one white hand and then the other, then laid down her gloves on the table, too. She picked up the rose in her fingertips and sitting on the wooden chair beside his bed, she held the rose tenderly for a moment to her, breathing its heavenly scent one last time, looking upon its beauty as she had so often before.

She held it there until the teardrops fell from her eyes onto its petals. They fell and rolled until they met, touched and became one with the raindrops that lay there.

As they did, Guylin's eyes began to move. Elzbet saw but was not sure, at first, if perhaps the firelight flickered on his face. But then his brow creased and his eyes twitched and opened. At first, he looked around as sightless as a newborn child until he turned his face to Elzbet. Then his eyes focused and he lay awake. He watched her for a while, then saw the rose. He weakly reached out to take it. Hesitant, she released it from her hand and he took it from her. He turned it back and forth in his fingers as he looked upon it.

The scent of it appeared to revive him until he found the strength to lift himself with effort from the bed and he sat.

At first, he lacked the strength to speak, but even so, he reached and took a tear from her cheek. He looked quizzically at the tear upon his finger, then took one from his own cheek. He parted his dry lips. Gently he spoke and said,

"In a thousand dreams, I have seen you cry, but I never saw one who cried for you. So I prayed, 'Let me cry my tears for her. Let each tear of mine redeem her from tears.'

"I made a silent pledge to take your pain, but it was a storm I could not weather. I thought that I would drown in the torrent. Yet if all of my tears spared you but one, I would wear each tear with pride, shed for you, and pray for strength to cry ten thousand more.

"I sought no prize, nor would I dare to ask a prize of you, but I was rewarded. Your face shone for me in all my darkness. Like a star to a sea-weary sailor, you guided me to still and calm waters."

His words had wearied him and Guylin fell silent. Elzbet said, "Then as your queen, I command you in this. I command you name your prize for your gift."

Guylin looked down, drew strength and replied, "Elzbet, you shame me. For my price is high. This passing world lacks gold to pay my wage. Let my eyes see the delight of your smile. Let my ears hear the laughter of your voice. My only prize? I name my prize Elzbet.

"Elzbet, I die, but by this rose, I swear that I love you. Always I have loved you. And by this rose, I swear again, my Elzbet, my Queen, I shall forever love you."

They looked first to each other and then to the rose that lay on the palm of his open hand. Without hesitation, Elzbet held out her hand. Silently, she placed her hand upon his, with the rose in between.

For a long while, they held their hands warm and closed, each around the other. And then, as one, they pressed their hands together until the thorns pricked their flesh, their bloods ran and met, and upon the rose's thorns, their blood mixed.

Chapter 18

The moon bathed the bridge that spanned the great northern river in silver light. Nothing moved on the bridge and no bird sang on the hillside. The only sound was the roar of the mighty mountain waters in the deep shadows below.

On the slopes of the hills above the bridge and along the ridges the men waited. Huddled together for warmth in groups of three and four, in dug out hollows beneath blankets and covers of woven branches and leaves, their breath steamed on the frosted grass. They had been waiting for most of the day. Some dozed while others lay watchful and awake, waiting for the signal, but none spoke. The order was for silence while they lay, waiting, waiting.

The road that led up from the trough to the bridge ran five miles between high banks, steep and clear, topped with woodland. In the camp in the valley below, sentries patrolled or warmed themselves by fires, waiting for the dawn, when they would begin the ascent, cross the bridge and then descend to the city that waited before them behind its thin walls.

Stars turned and the moon dipped in the sky. With the first chirp of birdsong and a faint light in the east, the sentries roused the men to break camp, while scouts rode out along the road to survey the bridge and then ride on to the way leading down to the city.

Those on watch on the ridges woke the sleepers when the first troop of scouts appeared. There were six riders on light horses trotting across the bridge, scanning with their eyes all around the road and above, but they did not see the men with blackened faces and blackened hands. As faint as the fading stars, the eyes of the watchers gazed patiently as the scouts rode by.

Time passed and the sky was growing pale. Now on the eastern landing of the bridge, more horsemen appeared, four men carrying flags and riding on heavy battle chargers and then their proud leader. He sat on a large and stout dappled horse, man and steed draped in heavy mail. There, they all waited, the warlord and his flagbearers, as his army arrived behind. Row after row they came, but none set foot or hoof upon the bridge.

Now no one slept on the ridges above the road. Men flexed cold fingers and ran them over their axe handles and bows, but they would not move until the signal came and the signal did not come yet.

For a long time, the arrogant warlord paced his horse back and forth until, at last, his scouts returned. The hooves rattled on the bridge as they approached their master to report. They spoke with him for several minutes, until finally, the warlord turned to his flagbearers. They raised their flags at his command and the horsemen began the ride across the bridge, first the flagbearers, then their leader and then his army behind him, until the clatter of hooves resounded like a roll of drums as they crossed the bridge over the deep, dark valley. Row upon row they came until they crossed the bridge. All the road was filled behind, and still they came.

Now, from the hilltop on the far side of the bridge, a trumpet blew and a flame shot up into the twilit sky. From beneath their covers, the men leapt out. All along the ridges, more fires were lit and more horns blew. A thousand axes swung with a fury and a vengeance to cut thick cords. Men lay hands on ropes and heaved, dislodging wedges from beneath great piles of logs and rocks that had lain for long years atop the steep banks, hidden beneath sods of earth and held back by the cords. The log piles groaned and the rocks and timbers began to roll down the slopes, gaining power and speed as they hurtled downwards. Great nets full of rocks in clefts above the narrow files released their load to tumble to the steep paths below.

The horses were first to take fright, shying up, some throwing riders from their backs, turning to flee, while other horses still came charging towards them. The invaders struggled in vain to control their panicking steeds as the first logs struck, crushing men, trapping their horses, while rolling rocks shattered legs. Beneath the bridge, huge bales of oil-soaked straw wrapped around the pillars burst into fire, sending tongues of flame leaping towards the bridge and lighting the valley, while men slid down ropes to escape to the valley below.

With the men who had lit the fires clear away, arrows began to rain down on the chaos of the bridge and upon the road shot from behind the shelter of hastily raised screens. A call went up to lift shields to defend against the volley of arrows that descended while the horses bucked and ran wildly, fleeing from the rising flames that raced along the ropes of the bridge on all sides and from the crushing logs on the road. Along the valley, horses bolted vainly to the woods where cords strung tight between boughs snapped riders from their backs, while nets clutched and tangled their hooves and brought them crashing to the ground.

Above the river, the officers of the ambush gave orders to waste no more arrows on the bridge where even now men leapt to their doom into the invisible waters of the icy river below or else were pushed there by crazed horses. They ordered to look instead for those who fled the road. The archers skipped like ghosts of shadow and smoke along the ridge, to spy out those who sought refuge by scrambling over the piles of maimed beasts, corpses and logs to try to escape. The fire that consumed the bridge lit their targets brightly as the archers stood black against the grey sky, took careful aim and bent their bows to resume the slaughter.

Far away from the bridge on the approaching road, the rear-guard listened in wonder to the shouts that came from ahead. They fidgeted and fretted, not knowing whether to advance to assist or to turn and retreat, until men came running wildly towards them screaming, "Flee! Flee for your lives! The land is bewitched! The forests march against us! Trees crush men!" Some shouted, "The earth swallows horses! Dismount and run for your lives!" While others came raving with tales of demons hiding in the tree tops, snatching men from the saddle as they rode and breaking their necks. "Devils fight against us!" they shrieked to men who dropped arms at their screams and ran in disarray and rout.

Throughout the morning twilight, the bridge burnt, and with the first rays of sun, it broke, sending flaming beams tumbling to the river below. The valley was filled with acrid smoke as the beams hissed, squealed and sent up billows of steam from the mountain river.

A rider was dispatched to report to the city. He rode with all speed until he came charging in the morning light down the road to the city gate, shouting at the top of his voice, "Victory! Victory at the bridge! Victory!"

The gates opened wide and the guards welcomed him in amazed delight. Breathless, he told his news. The enemy was shattered. Their horses were dead or captured and their engines lay smashed and smouldering on the road. Those that were left had fled to wander unprovisioned in the frigid and unforgiving mountains, to seek their way to their distant home or till hunger and mountain frost consume them.

The guards brought out a fresh horse and two companions were sent with him to the palace to tell the news to The Queen.

At the palace doors, they asked for The Queen, as they had great tidings, and they were told that The Queen had spent the night at the hospital, visiting the sick. The messenger was ordered first to wash his hands and face, then to go swiftly to tell Her Majesty. Four of the palace guards would ride with him to bring the joyous news.

The company soon arrived at the hospital by the gate. Outside the entrance, the carriage still waited in the street. The driver lay sleeping on the seat beneath a blanket.

Inside, Elysia sat in the reception hall downstairs with a doctor. They had sat there through the night. The messengers hurried in and said they must see The Queen without any delay. The doctor and Elysia led the men swiftly up the stairs and along the corridor to the door of Guylin's room.

They arrived just as The Queen was closing the door behind her to leave the room. The men stood still and waited for The Queen to address them, excited and eager to share their happy news. The Queen turned and looked at their faces, but instead of asking for word of the battle, she said to them simply, "Go and bury him with all the honour that befits the husband of a queen."

The men stood in silence and did not even say their news as The Queen walked past them to Elysia. She took her maid's hand and walked with her along the corridor, down the stairs and then to the carriage that waited outside. The driver sat up, removed his blanket and shook the reins.

Word was spreading throughout the town, people were coming out of doors and into the morning sunshine to hear the news. Some laughed in joy, some cried with relief, while others danced and embraced with gaiety and tears. The city would waken to a day of joy and jubilation, a day of freedom, a day of tranquillity and peace. The men would return in glory with their tales of the great night's adventures and their families and friends would welcome them home as heroes.

As the carriage rolled through the streets, some of the women recognised their queen's carriage and clapped in applause as she passed. Some in the bold exuberance of their joy even waved and blew kisses, but today, The Queen did not wave back.

Elzbet returned to the palace and took herself to her private rooms. She did not attend the celebrations that followed that day and that night, but her servants sent best wishes on Her Majesty's behalf.

Guylin was buried along with the rose, but The Queen did not attend his funeral. Throughout the entire term of her pregnancy, Elzbet stayed almost always indoors and away from sight, under the care and direction of her physician and attended by her maid. Elysia ran her mistress's errands and accompanied her at all her meals. Throughout all, The Queen dealt with pressing matters only, those that required her personal attention, making preparations and arrangements for the days ahead. All else, she delegated to her ministers and aides. She talked openly of many matters with her maid, save that she never discussed or even mentioned her feelings concerning her impending motherhood, and Elysia did not intrude to ask.

The summer fair of that year was delayed by a week to allow extra travelling time for merchants travelling from the east to arrive by the longer route over the small southern bridge. It would not be until the following year that the main road would be cleared and the great bridge rebuilt.

For nine months, Elysia scarcely left her mistress's side, until one afternoon whilst walking together in the palace garden, The Queen told her to fetch the midwife. Elysia ran and did as she was told.

Elysia waited with Darmid in a room downstairs, giddy and excited, anxious for news and barely able to sit still for a moment, while the midwife attended in an upper chamber. Darmid sat with one of his books. Elysia paced up and down, then sat down before him and asked boldly, "What will you say to My Lady when she comes down?" Darmid looked sombrely up from his book and said to her, "She will not be coming down."

Elysia, at first, frowned in incomprehension, then her eyes opened wide in horror. She dashed from the room and ran up the stairs, in tears as she ran. Sobbing for her mistress, Elysia ran till, at the door of the upper chamber, she heard the birth screams from within. Crying out for her mistress with all her strength, she was pulled away by order of the midwife, still screaming as they took her, whilst inside, The Queen gave birth to a boy. Elzbet embraced the child, kissed him with her loving tears and named him after his father, Guylin, before she died.

Elzbet was buried alongside Guylin. Their son was raised to be a king in a family that his mother had chosen for him, with brothers, sisters and a foster father and mother to love him. The Queen had appointed her brother as the boy-king's regent, which task he fulfilled truly and well.

Darmid was charged to supervise the boy's education, and so faithfully he did. When the boy reached an age of understanding, Darmid would often take him on walks in the hills, looking down on the city and kingdom which one day he would rule. There, on a crisp and clear autumn day, Darmid stood the boy upon a peak and told him to close his eyes and to listen to the wind.

The boy obeyed his teacher and dutifully closed his eyes, at first amused and then enrapt. When, at last, he opened his eyes and stood still in wonder, Darmid asked the boy, "What do you hear?"

"I hear two voices," he said, "and they tell me beautiful things. Who are they?"

Darmid took the boy's hand and led him from the heights. "They are your mother and your father," he said. "Now let me tell you a story."

And he told him the story of the Thunder Rose.

Now the harp's sounds fade and the tale is told.
The storyteller asks his listeners
"Was the princess pretty?" They all nod, "Yes."
"And was the knight strong, bravehearted and true?"
Again they nod. "And did he conquer all
For his lady love?" They nod, "Yes, he did."

The dark of night has come upon us now.
The embers of the fire glow beneath ash.
The watchmen of the city will escort
The girls to their homes in modest safety.

He takes his harp and plays another tune,
A song to lull the night to gentle sleep.
He will not rest for an hour or so yet.
He will mull over some troublesome phrase
Reconsider an episode or two
Ponder a tale for the following night
Perhaps a tale of adventure at sea
Or a loon's escapades. He sings softly

> *"If I could tell a tale of fire*
> *To fill the sky with light*
> *With words to soar upon the wings*
> *Of eagles in their flight*
> *I'd tell a tale to warm cold hearts*
> *With hope's eternal gleam*
> *A tale for all who lie at night*
> *Upon a bed and dream*
> *Of Thunder Rose!"*

The End